1 MONTH OF
FREE
READING

at

www.ForgottenBooks.com

By purchasing this book you are eligible for one month membership to ForgottenBooks.com, giving you unlimited access to our entire collection of over 1,000,000 titles via our web site and mobile apps.

To claim your free month visit: www.forgottenbooks.com/free835507

ISBN 978-0-364-71760-8
PIBN 10835507

THE SOUTHERN PLANTER

JANUARY
1908

THE SOUTHERN PLANTER PUBLISHING CO.

ESTABLISHED 1840 · RICHMOND, VIRGINIA.

VOL. 69

NO. 1

The Southern Planter.

DEVOTED TO

PRACTICAL AND PROGRESSIVE AGRICULTURE, HORTICULTURE, TRUCKING, LIVE STOCK AND THE FIRESIDE.

Agriculture is the nursing mother of the Arts.—XENOPHON.
Tillage and pasturage are the two breasts of the State.—SULLY.

69th Year. | **Richmond, Va., January, 1908.** | **No. 1.**

1 9 0 8.

Once again it becomes our pleasure to present to our readers the Annual Holiday Issue of The Southern Planter. We hope and believe that it will receive as warm a greeting as any previous issue, and more than this we cannot ask for it. We have striven to make it a fair sample of what we shall continue to send out to our subscribers each month of the year, except as to the cover. We are issuing a large edition of this number in excess of the requirements of our subscription list, and shall mail the extra copies to lists of farmers which we have secured from all over the territory covered by the regular subscribers to the Journal. We trust that the result of this may be a large addition to our subscription list. Each person to whom a sample copy is sent is requested to examine the same carefully and to see whether such a journal would not likely prove of great help to him in the pursuit of his calling, and further, he is desired to bring the same to the notice of his friends and neighbors and get them to join with him in subscribing for the paper. In this way he can secure the regular visits of the Journal each month for much less than the regular price of the same. Though the regular subscription price is only fifty cents per year—a price which no farmer can truthfully say he cannot afford—yet for $1.00 he can obtain the Journal for three years, or he can obtain it for himself and two friends for a year each for $1.00. We are anxious to increase our regular subscription list to 30,000 and, with the help of our regular subscribers and the wide circulation of this issue, we have every reason to hope that we shall accomplish this within the next three months. If only each of our regular subscribers would make it his business to send us in the name of one new subscriber—and many of them could readily send us a score with a few hours' work—the 30,000 list would be nearly doubled. We earnestly beg of them to take this opportunity of helping us. In this issue will be found all the regular Departments which it has been our custom to conduct for many years past. These deal with Farm Management, Garden and Orchard, Live Stock, Poultry, The Horse, and Miscellaneous topics of interest to farmers and, in addition, The Enquirers' Column. It is our purpose to continue these Departments in the future and, under the respective heads, to keep prominently before the farmers of the South Atlantic States every point essential to the profitable conduct of a farm in this section of the country. We do not aim to cover the whole United State with seasonable and pertinent advice for the conduct of farming operations. We do aim to give such advice and help as can be availed of by all farmers in the South Atlantic States and those immediately adjoining on the West. We are especially careful to so select the matter we publish that no farmer in the section named can fail to receive advice and help upon which he can confidently act. Whilst much of what we publish can be of service to farmers everywhere, as is evidenced by the fact that we have subscribers in every State of the Union and nearly every civilized country of the world who regularly renew their subscriptions and write highly complimentary letters as to the benefit derived, yet we base our claim to the support of Southern farmers on the fact that we especially cater to their conditions and deal with the crops peculiar to this section of the country. With such a purpose, and one so carefully observed, we do feel that we have an especial claim upon Southern farmers for their continued and extended support. In doing this work we have the constant help of such recognized authorities as Professor W. F. Massey, perhaps the most widely recognized authority on Southern agricultural problems, and who is, from a life-long experience, most closely familiar with all the problems confronting the Southern farmer, and is regarded by Southern farmers generally as one of the best friends they have ever had; and of Professor Soule, formerly Director of the Virginia Experiment Station, and now President of the Georgia State College of Agriculture, whose work amongst the Virginia farmers whilst he was with us gave him a strong hold upon their affections. These two gentlemen deal in each issue with the scientific questions affecting farm crops and live stock subjects and apply the principles deduced from scientific work to the daily problems of the farm and the live stock industry. Mr. Cal Husselman, perhaps the most expert practical poultryman in the country, gives the benefit of his life-long experience in handling poultry, not from the standpoint of the fancier, but from that of the poultry keeper, who keeps his flock for the benefit to be derived from it. Added to these, we shall now have also the help of Dr. Quick, the new Dean of the Agricultural Department of the Virginia Agricultural College at Blacksburg, a recognized authority on live stock husbandry, and also of Professor Saunders, the Professor of Dairy Husbandry at Blacksburg, and of other members of the staff of that College. Added to these, we have a large number of regular correspondents from amongst the practical farmers of the State, who give the results of their experience on the farm and teach valuable lessons based on their daily experiments and practice. Our own long experience on the farm before we took up the work of the Editorial chair enables us to add much to the work of these specialists and practical farmers in the way of adapting their lessons to the daily wants of our farmers, whilst our scientific training enables us to appreciate and apply the lessons taught. Nearly twenty years' occupancy of the position of Editor of this Journal has also put us in touch with the farmers of every section of the South, and we are able to turn for advice and help in every question which may arise to those most likely to be capable of giving the help needed, whilst our cordial and intimate relations with the Department of Agriculture at Washington, and with the staffs of the different Experiment Stations in the country gives us facilities for securing information on all matters affecting agricultural problems which cannot fail to be of constant service to our subscribers. Through the Enquirers' Column, and by letter, we answer hundreds of questions every year, and in the article on "Work for the Month" in each issue we strive to keep the farmers abreast of their work. Give us your support in this work with a generous hand. We deal generously with you. We promise you six hundred pages in the year. Last year we gave our subscribers a volume of 1,144 pages, and all this for fifty cents. In our advertising columns will be found everything wanted on the farm, offered by the most reliable parties, whose integrity we guarantee. If you have anything to sell, we can find you buyers. Let us hear from you quickly. Wishing all a prosperous and happy New Year.

OUR SUBSCRIPTION CAMPAIGN.

We would be very ungrateful indeed did we not thank our readers for the very lively interest they have taken in our Subscription Campaign, which is now well under way. Hundreds have sent us clubs, large or small, when renewing their own subscriptions, and we thank them most heartily. A great many more are now getting their lists ready, and to these we would suggest that in order to start with January issue they drop us a postal, notify-ing us about how many copies to save, and we will set them aside.

We will repeat the liberal offers and the rates published last month:

One dollar pays for a three-year subscription.

One dollar pays for two new subscriptions and the senders' also.

One dollar pays for The Southern Planter and Weekly Times-Dispatch one year.

One dollar pays for the Southern Planter and your county paper (if it is a $1 paper) one year.

Fifty cents pays for The Southern Planter and Farm and Fireside one year.

Fifty cents pays for The Southern Planter and Industrious Hen one year.

We wish also to repeat that we do not wish or expect our friends to work for us for nothing. It is to their financial advantage to avail themselves of one of the various clubbing offers and we will make it worth while to them if they will act as agents. Simply write for terms and samples.

Spotsylvania Co., Va., Dec. 14, 1907.

I think the Southern Planter one of the best papers of its kind I have ever read and do not want to miss a copy.
H. M. CLARKE.

Spotsylvania Co., Va., Dec. 12, 1907.

I have been taking the Southern Planter for one year and find that I cannot do without it. It is the most valuable farm paper I ever read. I look forward to its coming with great eagerness.
L. L. CORR.

Princess Anne, Co., Va., Dec. 2, 1907.

I think the Southern Planter far superior to any farm journal published, and I derive much valuable information from it.
CHARLES W. FRAZIER.

Burke Co., N. C., Dec. 4, 1907.

I like the Southern Planter. I take several farm papers, but I consider the Southern Planter the best. In fact, I don't see how it could be made any better.
M. R. RUDISILL.

Northumberland Co., Pa., Dec. 2, 1907.

While all the teachings of the Southern Planter do not apply to the Northern farmer, no farmer North or South should be without it.
E. M. REEDER.

Bedford Co., Va., Dec. 2, 1907.

I think the Southern Planter is far ahead of any other farm paper in the country, and I wish it all prosperity for 1908.
T. G. COLEMAN.

Worcester Co., Md., Dec. 14, 1907.

I take five farm papers and the Southern Planter is prized most of any of them.
A. C. HOLLOWAY.

Goochland Co., Va., Dec. 18, 1907.

I enjoy the Southern Planter and get much valuable information from same.
GEORGE A. PARSLEY.

Farm Management.

WORK FOR THE MONTH.

In our review of the results of the year's work on Southern farms in the December issue, we were unable to give more than an estimate of the yield of the cotton crop. We stated our belief that the crop would be materially less than that of the previous year. We are now in receipt of the official estimate of the crop, which is placed by the Department of Agriculture at 11,678,000 bales. This is as we estimated, a large reduction in the yield in the previous year, which was estimated at 12,500,000 bales. The crop this year was grown on about 32,000,000 acres, which makes the average yield about one-third of a bale to the acre. Even though cotton sold at a much higher price than it is now selling at, or than it sold at at any time last year, such a yield as this makes but a miserable poor return for the labor expended without allowing anything for the fertilizer. In no other branch of Southern agriculture is there more need for a radical change in methods than in cotton production. It has been demonstrated in hundreds of cases that a bale to the acre can be easily made on land of average fertility properly prepared and worked and more than twice this yield can be produced on rich land. The production of a bale to the acre would mean at present prices a fair return for the labor and fertilizer needed to produce the crop and would set at liberty over 20,000,000 acres of land upon which to produce other crops which we now buy in the markets of the world. The same or very little more labor would make the cotton crop of one bale to the acre which is now expended in making a third of a bale and the time saved in preparing and planting 20,000,000 acres in cotton could be used to produce corn, wheat, oats, hay and the leguminous crops on which to raise and feed cattle, sheep and hogs, the market for which products is always a good one and which, in the South, is at present supplied by the farmers of the North and West. The production of live stock would mean the improvement of the fertility of the land and therewith the capacity to make a heavy cotton crop on the reduced area at less cost for fertilizer. Thus while materially reducing land to be worked and thus saving money on the labor bill as large a cotton crop would be made, and this at much greater profit. Whilst there has already been a gratifying increase in the interest shown in live stock husbandry in the South yet there is room for an enormous increase in the production of meat in the South. We yet keep our meat-house sadly too often in the West and let the Western farmer make the profit on its production. We can make this meat at home cheaper than the Western man can make it and yet make a larger profit in doing so than he can, and can at the same time keep our money at home for improving our farms and homes.

The report on the area seeded to wheat during the fall months and its condition in December has just reached us. From this we find that there has been a reduction in the area sown as compared with last year of about 1 per cent.—equivalent to a decrease of 596,000 acres. The total acreage sown is 31,069,000. Maryland has sown 772,747 acres as against 796,646 acres sown last year. Virginia has sown 668,044 acres as against 674,792 sown last year. North Carolina has sown 583,251 acres as against a similar area last year. South Carolina has sown 328,128 acres as against a similar area last year. Tennessee has sown 840,430 acres as against 823,951 acres sown last year. Tennessee is therefore the only one of these Southern States showing an increased area seeded. West Virginia and Kentucky also show less area seeded. This decreased seeding is much to be regretted as we need to produce much more wheat in the South rather than less. We do not make our own bread in any of the Southern States and this is a serious reproach to us, as there is no reason whatever why we should not only do this but also make wheat for export. Probably the decrease in the area seeded this year is largely to be accounted for by reason of the late maturing of our summer crops owing to the cold spring and early summer. Farmers were too busy saving what had been made to get the land in order for wheat seeding. The condition of the seeded crop throughout the country is not at all satisfactory, as is stands only at 91 as against 94 a year ago and a ten-year average of 93. This decrease in the area sown and the low condition taken together would indicate that this year's winter wheat crop is not likely to be an average one. The failure of the wheat crop to increase in area which has now been a characteristic for several years when taken in conjunction with our enormous annual increase in population would seem to indicate that the days of this country as the great wheat exporting nation of the world are numbered and that very shortly we shall become dependent on some other nation for part of our daily bread. Either the profitable wheat lands are exhausted or the cost of production has so increased on the old lands as to make it a non-profitable crop at the average level of prices fixed by the world's production. Canada and the Argentine are now forging to the front as the great wheat-producing countries of this continent. They have both almost illimitable lands suited for the production of the crop and neither country has population to consume anything like even their present production. Argentina is now harvesting a magnificent crop of wheat which will all or nearly all be available for export. In the face of this we do not expect to see wheat advance much in value. Europe secured a very large share of our reserves from the crop of 1906 early in the fall of 1907 and can afford to wait for the Argentine, Indian and Australian crops. Notwithstanding this outlook, we are of opinion that we ought to grow more wheat in the South. It is a crop for which a market can be found right at home at a price which will pay the cost of production when the land is properly prepared for it and it has the great advantage of being a crop which can be put into the ground at a time when work does not heavily press on the farmer and it comes off here in the South in ample time to be followed by another crop to be harvested the same year. This crop should be a leguminous one and then the land will be in a better condition for further crops than if it had lain fallow all the year. The straw is always useful on the farm and when the price of the grain falls very low it can be profitably used for hog feeding mixed with corn and other grains. It is a crop which enables a much larger area of the farm to be kept under cultivation than is the case where only spring seeded crops are planted and it forms the basis of several of the best rotation in which profitable crops can be grown. Moreover, it is a crop which we need for home consumption in every household and of which at present we are large buyers from other sections of the country. There is no reason why we should not grow from 25 to 30 bushels of wheat to the acre profitably. In England last year the yield was 35 bushels to the acre and the average yield in that country for 10 years is 32 bushels to the acre.

The winter oat crop is looking well where the seed was sown early, but this was the case in few places for the same reason that caused the reduction in the area of wheat sown. We expect to learn that there is a much less area of winter oats sown than for several years. We would urge that the area be supplemented by the seeding of oats in February and March. For this spring seeding we would advise the use of the Appler or Burt oat, both of which varieties are giving excellent results in the South. Begin the preparation of the land for the seeding of this spring crop as soon as ever the land is dry enough to work. Much of the want of success in growing spring oats in the South is to be attributed to the use of varieties of seed not adapted to our climate and to the poor preparation of the land before seeding. Merely plowing the land is not sufficient. It must not only be well and deeply plowed, but the land must then be finely broken by cultivators repeatedly before seeding and if the soil be lacking in available fertility, acid phosphate should be applied at the rate of 250 or 300 pounds to the acre, or farm yard manure be liberally applied and worked into the land. This will be more effective if supplemented by 100 or 200 pounds to the acre of acid phosphate. Oats will pay for liberal fertilization as well as any other crop. If farm yard manure is to be used the sooner it is put into the land the better.

Whilst the weather keeps mild top-dress the wheat and winter oats with farm yard manure. The manure spreader is the best means of doing this work as it puts the manure on in a fine condition and spreads it evenly over all the land and this is more essential than a heavy coating to secure good results. Every farmer ought to have a manure spreader who keeps at least ten head of stock. It will save its cost in increased results in two years' time. Where no manure spreader is available, take pains to break the manure finely and spread it evenly. The coarsest, freshest manure should be got out on to the land intended to be put into corn. Haul it from the barns as made and then it is only once to handle and it will leach where the leachings will be absorbed and do good.

Keep the plows running whenever the land is dry enough to work well and do not be afraid to turn up two or three inches of the subsoil. The winter will disintegrate and aerate this new soil and make it fitted to produce crops in the summer. Turn the furrows on edge and do not throw them completely over and flat. This will enable the old and new soil to be mixed easily with the harrow and cultivator. Plow all the land. Don't miss a few inches between each furrow, and plow it all to an even depth.

See to it that new fences are built and old ones repaired. Make all fences straight as nearly as possible so that there may be no corners into which you cannot take the plow and harrow.

Ditches should be opened and drains put in where needed. Let these be put down deep and see that they are straight and have sufficient fall to carry off all the water quickly.

Have plenty of long feed stored in the barn or convenient thereto so that if we should have a heavy snow storm the stock will not suffer nor will you be compelled to haul in feed in a frozen or wet condition.

Fill the ice-house at the first opportunity. It is never safe in the South to wait for thick ice. Very often here the first is the last opportunity to secure ice.

Keep the wood pile well replenished. We often get a spell of hard weather in January and wood is then needed badly.

When the weather is unfit for outdoor work clean, repair and paint the implements, wagons, tools, harness and have them all in good order for work when wanted.

In the evening plan out the rotation of crops to be planted in the spring and so arrange these that they will work in well with each other and not crowd the teams or labor to handle them at the best time.

Take an inventory of everything on the farm and put a fair value on each article and enter in a book and then open a cash account and every day enter every item of cash received and paid and goods sold and bought and thus be able at the end of the year to see how you have prospered. It is also well to keep an account with every crop and the stock so that you may know what each costs and then you can tell at what price you must sell in order to make a profit. Every merchant does this and then fixes his selling price accordingly. Farmers are always complaining that the "other fellow" fixes the price on his products. This will always be the case until the farmer knows what each article he has to sell has cost him. When he knows this he can fix his own price and justify it and will then come much nearer getting it. Don't forget in making up the account that you live rent free and get much of what you eat from the farm. Credit the farm with a full price for these items. If you had to pay money out for them you would find that they came to a good round sum each year.

ROTATION OF CROPS.

Editor Southern Planter:

There is no subject connected with farming more important than that of crop rotation, and I wish to commend the rotation suggested by Mr. Hicks in the last number of the Planter. I think, however, he is wrong when he expresses the opinion that rye will not pay as a cover crop after corn. It is true that rye will add no nitrogen to the soil and should be turned under before it has made much growth or it will remove too much moisture. It will do nothing but conserve fertility; it will aid in holding what the soil gains during Mr. Hick's excellent rotation. I know that the Planter has pointed out time and time again the harmfulness of leaving a field bare during the winter, but it is slow work driving a new idea home. You may persuade a farmer to adopt a sensible rotation as long as he gets something off the land but he can't appreciate a loss unless it is visible to the eye. In raising a heavy weight it is good to make a long pull, a strong pull and a pull all together but it is quite as important to hold what you have gained. Rye is the hold-fast and by all means should be included in Mr. Hick's rotation. One question—will the double-action harrow, without plowing, suitably prepare the land for cow peas or soja beans?

Bedford Co., Va.   M. A. CROCKETT.

Either the double-action harrow or a disc harrow will effectually prepare the stubble land for a crop of cow peas or soja beans. It should be run lengthwise and across the field.—Ed.

LAND IMPROVEMENT.

Editor Southern Planter:

After reading the article of Prof Massey and your editorial note thereon in the last issue, I feel impelled to an expression on this subject, although greatly in fear that I shall only illustrate the proverb that "fools rush in where angels fear to tread." As I understand Prof. Massey, he claims that even where every pound of grain and roughage grown on the farm is consumed by live stock, and the manure carefully saved and returned to the soil, there must be a gradual loss of phosphoric acid and potash, the same being carried off by milk or meat, eggs, butter or whatever products leave the place. In other words every farmer must eventually become a buyer of both phosphoric acid and potash or reconcile himself to leaving a poorer farm than he inherited from his predecessors. This is a question which has often occurred to me and one that is hard to answer. Theoretically, Prof Massey is right and he can prove his position by figures; for unless there is an inexhaustible supply of the necessary mineral elements in the soil, it must eventually become depleted.

The question which confronts us resolves itself into this: Is the supply of phosphoric acid and potash inexhaustible? and capable of treatment to make it perennially available? Or is it not? And I think it is about the most important one that confronts humanity.

In view of our present experience it is possible to throw a little light on this subject, from both points of view. In the first place, all will admit that it is possible to take any piece of land rich in mineral elements, and to grow corn or wheat on it year after year and by so doing exhaust the available phosphoric acid and potash, as indicated by the gradual decrease in the yield, until it gets to a point beyond which it does not pay to cultivate; but the experiments at Rothamstead, and in fact the observation of every intelligent farmer goes to show that after a while land so treated gets into a state where it will not deteriorate any further; in other words, where the annual loss of mineral constituents is so small that the natural process of soil weathering, brought about by cultivation, will balance it, and the land will go on producing its minimum crop indefinitely, the only variation being due to climatic conditions favorable or otherwise to the crop. That this is the case on the vast majority of land will be pretty generally conceded, and the fact that the amount of grain produced will be so small as to make its cultivation unprofitable does not bear upon the argument that here is land that is perennially fertile. There is another point that I desire to establish in order to perfect my premises, and that is that all land will not deteriorate to the same point; some will go as low as a few bushels of corn or wheat per acre, some will stop at two bushels of the former and 4 or 5 bushels of the latter per acre, the experiments at Rothamstead seem to point to 12 bushels of wheat as the minimum under their conditions of soil and climate and the question has never, so far as I know, been decided as to the determining factor, whether it was lack of phosphoric acid, or nitrogen.

If we admit, then, that all lands have a state of minimum production beyond which point they will not go under conditions of proper cultivation, and that lands differ in their productive capacity after reaching this point, the important thing to find out is first the cause of this difference and second the remedy to apply in order to bring the poorer lands up to the standard of the best lands. Here is a problem quite as abstruse as any that is engaging the attention of the scientists at our Experiment Stations, and one which, if solved on a commercial basis within reach of the average agriculturist, would be of as great benefit to the American farmer as any that can engage the attention of the philantropist.

Soil analysis seems to show that the supply of phosphoric acid and potash in the average land is far in excess of the needs of any crop, no matter how luxuriant, but that something is lacking to make it available, and now, that we have hastily reviewed the known, let us turn to the field of conjecture.

My own experience on a run-down farm would seem to indicate that nitrogen was the lacking element, for the growth of legumes alone, without manure or fertilizer, will make an improvement in most of the lands that have come under my observation in Virginia. If this is the case, then by alternating corn and peas, or common clover and wheat, on the same land that produces five bushels of wheat or two barrels of corn as its minimum crop, we should increase that yield a little, and I believe this will generally be the case even without the addition of one pound of commercial fertilizer or manure of any sort; a steady rotation which follows every cereal crop with a legume must eventually carry the land up to another and increased point of productivity. We will say for argumentative purposes four barrels of corn and ten bushels of wheat, and maintain it there for a considerable period. How long this state of affairs will last I am unable to say. According to Prof Massey's theory such a rotation should impoverish the land of its mineral constituants quite as rapidly as the steady cultivation of a cereal crop; for although the crop of grain is only removed bienniallly, it is about twice as large as the annual crop where no legume is grown and therefore removes the same amount of phosphoric acid and potash from the soil at the expiration of every two year period. In consequcnee the only gain to the farmer is the hay made from the leguminous crop, which will be generally found about as profitable as the grain sold from the cereal crop in all localities which do not produce hay for export.

Under this system, if the above figures are correct, there is a distinct gain in the productive powers of the land without the application of either phosphoric acid or potash, brought about by a two-year rotation in place of annual cropping. The query naturally arises from whence comes this additional production and the answer, in view of the present state of our knowledge, must be from the nitrogen accumulation which the leguminous crop has taken from the atmosphere, thereby going to show that our poor lands contain naturally as much available phosphoric acid and potash as is necessary to balance the nitrogen content gathered from the atmosphere, and that the first step on the road to improvement should be the cultivation of a legume to precede each cereal rather than the purchase of chemical fertilizers of any sort.

It is my opinion that any farmer who is making his living cultivating land of only moderate fertility and who annually puts in a fixed acreage of corn producing from two to four barrels per acre may, by cutting that acreage down to one-half the customary amount, and sowing the other half in peas, and each year growing corn on the pea stubble and peas on the corn stubble, eventually grow as many barrels of corn per annum as he did when planting all the land to corn; or, in other words, he will grow twice as many bushels of corn per acre and have the pea hay cut from half his land as a clear gain over and above the cost of the seed and harvesting. Whether or not the establishment of a longer rotation extending over a period of three, four or more years would not in the long run carry the productive capacity of most soils still higher, is a question upon which I have no positive data, and in fact the only way to settle these points is the plan adopted at Rothamstead, where a lifetime—and that a very long one, now over seventy years—has been devoted to the cultivation of experimental plots on different plans, and a careful record kept of each experiment.

To sum up, then, I will say that it is my belief that land may be positively improved by the growth of legumes alone, even where most of the grain is sold from the farm, and that where all the grain, hay, straw, fodder, etc., is fed to live stock and the manure returned to the soil, there will be a rapid increase of fertility without the purchase of commercial fertilizers of any sort, and that while I am open to conviction to the contrary, I should be very sorry to be obliged to think otherwise, as to do so would be to abandon all hope of agricultural success except that purchased at the expense of our less fortunate associates in this line of industry.

Mathews Co., Va.   PERCIVAL HICKS.

FERTILIZERS IN THE CENTRAL WEST.

Editor Southern Planter:

One of the most interesting bulletins we have lately received is from the Purdue University Agricultural Experiment Station of Indiana. It is entitled, "The Use of Fertilizers on Southern Indiana Soils." In one table it is shown that a complete fertilizer, or one containing nitrogen, phosphoric acid and potash, increased the crop of wheat in 1903 eight bushels per acre; nitrogen and potash, without phosphoric acid, increased the crop one bushel; nitrogen and phosphoric acid increased the crop two bushels, and phosphoric acid and potash, without any nitrogen, increased the crop six bushels. The profit in this last application, after paying for the fertilizer, was $3.84 per acre. The complete mixture added but two bushels to the crop over the application of phosphoric acid and potash alone, and as the nitrogen probably cost as much as both the other ingredients, it was evident that it was not used at a profit. The plots receiving nitrogen and phosphoric acid and nitrogen and potash both showed a very small increase. This shows what I have often insisted upon—that tests of phosphoric acid and potash separately do justice to neither, for of all the plant foods used by crops these two work in harmony more than any other, and are necessary one to the other for the best results. Another point I have often dwelt upon, and that is that in farming in a short rotation with legumes brought in often there will never be any need for the purchase of any nitrogen on a grain farm. The bulletin says: "By turning under the legume crops, the grain crops and other non-legume crops are able to secure the nitrogen necessary for their growth from that present in the decaying legume material. This affords by far the cheapest source of nitrogen for such crops. As a matter of fact, it is

First Prize, 2-Year-Old Holstein-Friesian Bull at Virginia State Fair, 1907. Owned by Mr. George M. Carpenter, Wilkes-Barre, Pa.

very doubtful if it would pay to feed nitrogen in the shape of commercial fertilizer to grain crops, particularly corn. A seventy-five bushel crop of corn and stalks removes about one hundred and forty pounds of nitrogen from the soil. As this is worth, in the form of commercial fertilizer, at present prices, about twenty cents per pound, it will be seen that there is about $28.00 worth of nitrogen in a seventy-five bushel crop of corn, and as it is impossible to recover all the nitrogen supplied in the form of fertilizer, it would take considerably more than this amount to produce seventy-five bushels of corn. As a matter of fact, it can be seen that it will be absolutely necessary to resort to the use of legumes or some cheaper source of nitrogen than that of commercial fertilizers if corn production is to be profitably maintained on our soils.

In an address I made at the Normal Farmers' Institute of Pennsylvania, at Clearfield, in May, 1906, I took the stand that where a farmer whose interest is in grain or cotton, farms in a short rotation and brings in legume crops frequently on his land and feeds them, and saves the manure, he can keep his soil improving and never buy an ounce of nitrogen in any form. Some considered the statement rather broad, but every year the experiments at the Stations continue to show that on the corn crop especially it never pays to buy a complete fertilizer, and it is getting more and more evident that the same is true of the wheat crop. The men on the eastern shore of Maryland who have brought their lands up to the average of forty bushels of wheat per acre are the ones who years ago abandoned the purchase of nitrogen altogether and are using only acid phosphate and potash.

Another interesting item in this Indiana bulletin is the statement in regard to the relative value of floats or pulverized raw rock and the dissolved rock or acid phosphate. In 1906 an application of 1,000 pounds of the raw phosphate rock increased the corn crop twenty bushels per acre, while an application of 715 pounds of acid phosphate, costing the same amount of money, made an increase of five bushels less than the raw rock. On the wheat crop the first season the acid phosphate was away ahead, but in two years thereafter the rock was ahead, showing that it was slower in coming into availability. If used in connection with stable manure or with a sod turned under for corn, I believe that the floats will be the cheaper. The way that soil holds on to phosphoric acid was well shown by an application three years before the corn crop, nothing having been applied in the meantime. The check plot made eighteen bushels per acre; the plot where acid phosphate had been applied three years before made thirty-three bushels per acre, and where rock floats had been applied three years before the crop was thirty-eight bushels per acre. At the Rothamsted Station in England, where 1,150 pounds of commercial fertilizer have been applied annually for fifty years, the average crop of wheat grown continuously on the land has been thirty-seven bushels per acre, and has been as high as forty-five bushels, while on another piece, where fourteen tons of stable manure have been applied every year for fifty years and wheat grown continuously, the average crop has been thirty-six bushels per acre and the highest forty-two bushels. This would seem to indicate that fertilizers will maintain the productivity of the land, leaving profit out of view.

The bulletin recommends for the Southern Indiana soils 1. "The feeding of as much of the produce grown on the land as possible and the return of the manure to the soil. 2. The practice of a systematic rotation of crops containing one or more of the legume crops in the series. 3 The liberal use of clover, cow peas or other legume crops is considered essential in order to keep up the nitro-

First Prize Dutch Belted Bull, Virginia State Fair, 1907. Owned by Mr. G. H. Dodge, Wilkinsonville, Mass.

gen supply and keep the soil in good mechanical condition.

The readers of this Journal will bear me out in saying that these are the very points I have been hammering at for many years. It all comes back to the fact that humus-making material is essential to the maintenance of the productivity of the soil, and when we can combine the nitrogen fixation with the humus-making we have reached the point where we can dispense with the nitrogen of the fertilizer manufacturer. I believe that it will be found in the long run that the use of phosphate rock finely pulverized will be found more profitable than the use of acid phosphate with the danger of depriving the soil of lime carbonate through its use, and the consequent souring of the soil. In a short rotation, where legume crops are frequently grown, the manure from feeding them and all the roughage and some of the grain raised carefully saved, and applied as fast as made, the soil will rapidly increase in humus and, with a soil abounding in humus, the pulverized floats can be profitably used, and will furnish phosphoric acid in greater supply for the same money than acid phosphate will and, having the phosphorus in the soil, it will stay there till some crop calls for it. Hence, in the permanent improvement of the soil the floats will be a profitable investment. But floats applied to land from which the humus has been worn out will be very slow in making any returns, and until there is a considerable improvement in the humus content of the soil it will be better to use the acid phosphate, and the place where this and potash will pay best in the improvement of the soil is on the pea crop that will give you forage and humus-making material. Feed the legumes liberally with the mineral plant foods and you can depend on their doing the rest.

W. F. MASSEY.

FACTORS AFFECTING THE CORN CROP.

(Continued from the December Issue.)

Editor Southern Planter:

Time of Cutting.

The effect of cutting corn at different stages of growth is a matter of considerable importance, especially where the elevations are high and frost is likely to fall at an early date. To test this matter, Early Leaming corn was cut at two different stages of growth. The yield of grain in bushels was 36.50 with the early cut plat, and 38.29 bushels with the late cut plat. The per cent. of grain was 81.80 with the early cut sample, and 82.69 with the late cut sample. There was thus not a marked difference between the two cuttings. What the effect of early harvesting would be on the germinating and productive powers of the crop through a series of years cannot be determined unless a test of this kind were continued for a number of years. In the face of danger from early frosts, comparatively early cutting—that is, when the kernels are glazed and the grain hardening—may be resorted to without serious loss.

Fodder Corn.

To determine the best method of growing fodder corn, three plats were seeded so as to leave 20,000, 30,000 and 40,000 stalks per acre, respectively. The corn was sown in drills 39.6 inches apart, and 4, 6 and 8 inches in the drill row, respectively. The yield of cured fodder in 1905 and 1906 was largest from the 20,000 stalks, the average for both years being 3.99 tons. The smallest yield followed the closest planting, or 3.03 tons. The test indicates that 20,000 plants would be about the right number to use where a maximum yield of fodder is sought.

Fertilization of the Corn Crop.

The fertilization of the corn crop is a very important matter. All indications point to the fact that an occasional turning under of green crops or the application of farm yard manure and such supplemental fertilizers as the type of soil manifestly needs will certainly increase the yield of corn, which is a desideratum of the greatest importance, owing to the low average yields secured at present. Tests with fertilizers have therefore been under-

"Lucky Pride II.," First and Champion Shorthorn Bull at Virginia State Fair, 1907; 3 Years Old; Weight About a Ton. Owned by Mr. Frank W. Cotton, Manilla, Ind.

taken, and while the work has only been in progress one year, some deductions seem justifiable, and it is certainly

not improper to present the data secured for the consideration of all who are interested in this question, as it cannot fail to reveal some facts of fundamental importance which can be put in practice with excellent results by the average farmer.

Sixty plats were devoted to the work, twenty in each of the three ranges. On the first range cow peas were ploughed under in the fall of 1905 and the ground seeded to winter barley, which was ploughed under in the spring of 1906. On the next range cow peas were ploughed under in the fall of 1905, and the land received no other treatment. On the third range wheat was sown in the summer of 1905, and the stubble was turned under in the fall of the same year and received no further treatment. The seed bed in all three instances was carefully prepared.

There were twenty plats in each range, to which eighteen forms or combinations of fertilizer were applied, two being reserved as check plats and receiving no fertilizer. Notice that acid phosphate, Thomas slag, and floats were compared. Lime was used at the rate of one ton per acre together with mixed fertilizers, varying in amounts from 225 to 450 pounds per acre. Decidedly larger yields of fodder were obtained from the range where cow peas and barley and cow peas alone were ploughed under than from either of the others. The largest yield of fodder was obtained on the cow pea range, due, no doubt, to the readiness with which pea vines decay and render up their store of plant food in an available form. One would not have expected the plants to be so vigorous on the wheat range. Where the two crops were ploughed under better returns might have been anticipated, and in a favorable season, no doubt, larger yields would have followed. On the plats where an abundance of nitrogen was supplied in the form of green manure but little benefit was obtained from fertilizers. In most instances they failed to show any marked benefit. Where wheat alone was ploughed under the increase from the use of fertilizers was remarkable, indicating very clearly that putting the land in perfect mechanical condition and supplying it abundantly with humus through the turning under of leguminous crops is one of the surest and best ways of increasing its crop-yielding powers and effecting a saving in commercial fertilizers.

The results indicate what would naturally be expected —that applications of farm yard manure and the ploughing under of green leguminous crops constitutes one of the essentials in increasing crop production at a moderate cost; that, next to this, the addition of phosphates would be advisable at the rate of 150 to 300 pounds per acre, and that acid phosphate would seem to furnish this in the cheapest form. It also seems advisable to use muriate of potash in moderate quantities. The results show that a combination of this kind would result in a considerable increase in the yield of corn at a moderate cost per bushel. Where liberal applications of complete fertilizers are used on land poorly supplied with vegetable matter, a substantial increase may be anticipated, but the cost would be greater in every case. A careful study of the data should enable the more intelligent and successful fertilization of the corn crop in the future, and induce the farmer to use green crops more freely to supply the needed nitrogen and change the mechanical and physical condition of his soil to one corresponding more nearly with the requirements of such a rapidly growing crop as corn.

Effect of Change of Location.

We have demonstrated that the choicest types of thoroughbred Western corn, when brought to this section, are changed materially during a single season of growth, owing to the readiness with which corn adapts itself to a new environment. By using the native corn for mother plants and the eastern seed as a source of pollen, it was thought that desirable changes could be brought about much more readily than by bringing in thoroughbred Western seed and attempting to adapt it to a new environment. The value of this method seems to be justified by our results, and the practice involved to effect improvement is so simple that it can be adopted on any farm and, if systematically pursued by all our corn growers for a year or two and rigid selection followed thereafter, the yield can unquestionably be increased quite markedly for a comparatively small out lay in the beginning.

The variety selected wsa a local strain of Leaming corn, which had been grown on the College farm for many years without any definite attempt at selection. The ear was very solid, but the strain was lacking in uniformity, desirable type of ear, and depth of grain. The average measurement of twenty ears indicated that the length of twenty-five grains was about 11.29 inches, and the per cent. of protein about 8.38. The plan of improvement was as follows: A thoroughbred strain of the same variety was obtained from the West. The ears of this corn were larger and more uniform in type and the grains were of greater depth. The work was carried on with forty ears, twenty ears of the local and twenty ears of the improved strain being used. These ears were numbered from one to forty, the native corn was given the odd numbers, and the Western corn the even numbers. The ears were all planted in separate rows in the breeding plat in regular order from one to forty, so that in no case were two ears of the same strain of corn planted side by side. A piece of uniform land was surveyed off, making exactly two-thirds of an acre. Each ear occupied a space of 10x100 links, or 1-100 of an acre. The seed was planted in hills 39.6 inches in each direction and two stalks were left to the hill.

A review of the data presented indicates that starting with not more than forty ears of corn it would be possible, through selection, to obtain an unlimited number of strains, all presenting some of the characteristics of a given variety and yet, withal, possessed of striking differences as to the character and shape of the ear, the size, shape and quality of the grain, the straightness of the rows, the covering of the butt and tip, the firmness of cob and grain, size and character of stalk, earliness and lateness, per cent. of grain to cob and total crop, number of grains per ear, and the weight per individual ear. These are but a few of the physical variations that appear in working with a comparatively small number of ears of corn of a variety that has been in existence and supposedly standardized for years and years.

These facts show that to effect evolution by this method it is necessary to isolate the particular individual possessed of those special qualities sought. This is a more difficult undertaking than is generally thought to be the case, but when the right ears are located, one is then in position to go forward through systematic selection and perpetuate a sort that will give increased yields and possess many useful characteristics not transmitted with uniformity by what are regarded as pure strains of the variety. It must be apparent to all that the strain of corn has a wonderful effect on its utility, and that thousands of strains are on the market of supposedly standard breeding which fall far below the requirements of that variety, and it is due to this fact that there is such a strife over their use in many localities, for it has been demonstrated on our experimental plats that several strains of a given variety grown even in a single state possess widely different characteristics, some desirable and some equally objectionable. The choice of a strain, therefore, is a matter of serious concern, as it now appears that the progeny of only three ears out of all those so carefully selected and tested in our breeding plat are worthy of permanent preservation and selection, yet the work involved in two years in handling and recording the qualities of hundreds of ears has been enormous.

The yield varied with the forty ears in 1905 from 28.14 to 57.26 bushels, a difference of 29.12 bushels. Two season's work shows that some of the ears have the ability of transmitting their desirable qualities while others vary widely. Out of the whole lot there are only three strains which impressed us as worthy of perpetuation These were ear No. 11, which made a yield of 46.53 bushels in 1905 and 72.99 bushels in 1906; ear No. 23, which made a yield of 41.73 bushels in 1905 and 78.46 bushels in 1906; and ear No. 35, which made a yield of 54.94 bushels in 1905 and 81.69 bushels in 1906. Notice that these three ears made a substantial increase in the yield per acre the second year from planting, and they have retained all the desirable characteristics of the original ears planted, together with the grafted quality of high yields and uniformity in type and ability to transmit the most valuable qualities from one generation to another.

The foregoing data is presented for the study of the corn grower, and if he will follow some of the deductions which may properly be drawn from the work, he will learn much that will be helpful to him, and it will do more for the permanent betterment of the corn crop than anything else, because it will convince him of the wide variability of corn under different conditions, of the individual characteristics, good and bad, which are evidenced, and the fact that the master of the situation—that is, the trained human being—can dominate it and increase or decrease, add to or take away from the desirable and undesirable qualities of the corn plant, and so materially affect the yield of his crop if he undertakes the work intelligently.

ANDREW M. SOULE.

(To be continued.)

CORN FODDER AND LIME.

Editor Southern Planter:

I am in hearty sympathy with your campaign for the careful saving of the whole of the corn crop. I believe that in every part of our section the entire plant is worth

THE SOUTHERN PLANTER.

handling—both with a view to securing the greatest possible feeding value, and also to return this vegetable matter to the soil in the form which gives it the greatest value as a fertilizer. This means that the crop must be cut and shocked before the blades are over-ripe, and that whether husked by machinery or not the stover must go through some cutting or shredding process before it goes into the bedding and manure pile.

I am thankful that in my own vicinity the wasteful, time-killing fashion of topping and stripping the fodder in the field is practically a thing of the past, and many men are drawing the line on filling manure with the uncut and uneaten stalks. Where stalks are fed in racks in the barn yard and the refuse thrown under foot all winter, freezing and thawing as may be, they will not be sufficiently rotted to spread easily until well into the next summer, and this means that they will probably not get on the land in time to benefit the crops of the year following the winter in which fed except at a great expense of labor in forking and spreading.

There are, however, two sentences in your editorial on page 955 which seem to need further explanation or qualification. You say: "In the corn crop, nearly half the value is in the fodder, and to waste this by leaving it in the field to bleach and blow away is criminal negligence." There is no doubt about the negligence, but should we not say that in the average poor crop of 18 or 20 bushels per acre, nearly one-half the value is in the fodder? I am very certain the dairymen in the region around Washington, who feed all their stover and sell timothy hay, will not agree that the stover is worth anywhere near as much as the corn in their crops which run from 40 to 80 bushels shelled corn per acre, and this is the sort of corn we must all be aiming for.

Again you say "Good, well-secured fodder is as good feed for stock as timothy hay, and will make quite as good returns in milk or meat, and especially is this so where it is finely shredded." The blades, husks, and possibly the smaller part of the stalk above the ear taken together are perhaps equal in value to a like quality of average timothy hay, but the value of these parts is not increased by shredding, and it seems to be the conclusion of much careful experimental work that no amount of mechanical preparation will make the hard stalk, shell and pith below the ear a valuable stock food, as the effort necessary for its digestion seems to equal its nutritive power.

One of our best farmers who had begun on naked land at the close of the war, and who has developed a farm which would be a credit to any section of our country, a practical dairyman keeping more cows than he could raise grain to feed, yet always having surplus forage for sale, explained his experience and practice thus: "I have the shredder come every fall and I haul up to the barn and have husked and shredded by the machine as much of the crop as I can store on top of all the hay mows, and in every spare space in the barn. I have the rest of the crop husked from the shock by hand and feed the bundle fodder in a rack in the barn yard on all good days when the cows are out. I don't think they eat the shredded fodder a bit closer than they do the long stalks. I'm not sure they eat it as close, but the pith and refuse is the nicest bedding for cows in stanchions that I ever had,

and makes the best absorbent in the gutters. It is much better than straw, and I can bale my wheat straw and ship it, and a car of straw will buy a car of lime." This opinion of shredded fodder is supported by the Experiment Stations of both Maryland and Illinois. Shredding is worth its cost for convenience in handling, and as a means of saving and spreading the liquid manure, and the cutting of the fodder into four or six-inch lengths is nearly as good, but neither process adds anything to the food value of the stalks, nor to their palatability. Again, shredded or fine cut dry fodder kept in tight buildings usually gets too dry and harsh to be relished towards the latter part of winter. The well-built fodder rick still has its place in good and scientific farming—the silo having a province of its own and the husker and shredder a special mission.

Lime in Small Amounts.

And now I would like to lend my support to the rational use of lime as a means of improving our Southern soils. Here again the experiments which I have followed by the publications of various stations, and my own experience, teach me to be very conservative. I am very positive in my conviction that most of our land needs lime, but I am convinced that a very moderate amount will often have just as marked and beneficial an effect as a heavy application.

When we advocate a ton of lime per acre we are simply closing the question of liming for the man with a large farm ten miles or even five miles from a railroad. He simply cannot afford in a majority of cases to purchase and haul such a quantity, and by leading him to suppose that he must use this amount on his thin plow land in order to enable it to produce grass or clover, we are directly encouraging him to keep on plowing and skinning with the aid of a little mixed fertilizer.

When I can exactly suit myself I apply 600 pounds of freshly burned lime per acre. This is finely ground and sacked in 200 pound sacks. If kept beyond ten days or two weeks there will be enough slacking to burst some of the sacks and if left unused indefinitely all the sacks will burst and the lime become fully air-slacked. However, lime can be handled more easily and with less discomfort when in this form than when in bulk.

To distribute 600 or 800 pounds evenly over an acre requires either a drill or a very careful man. I have had a man who would do it by emptying the sacks one by one in the wagon and spreading with shovel, throwing only a quart or two at a time, and always with the breeze. It is best to blanket the horses, and if by chance any lime gets on them be sure that it is thoroughly brushed out of the hair before they get wet, or permanent injury will result. However the lime is applied the men will need to use vaseline or grease on all exposed parts of their hands and faces, and a damp handkerchief tied over nose and mouth is a great help.

Any man who works in fresh lime will realize that it is a more active chemical agent than anything he has ever put on his hand with the possible exceptions of nitrate of soda and muriate of potash, and no one thinks of using a ton per acre of these substances.

I never had a successful crimson clover patch sown in field corn until I tried it on land limed in the spring, and

I have never missed a catch on land so treated. We now have crimson clover growing for a fourth successive season on land which has produced corn every year. This is pine stump land of naturally thin quality and quite acid. The first season the corn was almost nothing and crimson clover failed to stand. The next spring a liming as above indicated was given, resulting in paying corn and good clover, and as stated, the fourth clover crop is now on the land with no further liming. Some floats, however, was sown last spring.

In one or two cases I have followed the limed corn with oats and red clover, and so far have not failed to secure a stand. I was somewhat skeptical on the subject of liming until I began trying it. Now I am enthusiastic in advocating a small application. The one time I tried a half ton or more I also tried about 600 pounds per acre of dissolved rock on the same crop of corn, and could not have had a worse failure if I had planted the corn alone. I will go slowly hereafter in applying fertilizer with the lime.

I prefer to lime the corn crop in order that it may be thoroughly mixed with the soil, and the corn is almost invariably benefitted, but the primary object of liming is to insure grass, especially the clovers, and cow peas. I would never lime anything but a swamp if I intended to cultivate it continuously without any hay or cover crops.   W. A. SHERMAN.

Vienna, Fairfax Co., Va.

The statement made and to which exception is taken that "nearly half the value is in the fodder" is substantially correct. The exact distribution as determined by many analyses is 60 per cent. in the ear and 40 per cent. in the stover (digestible matter). Whether these exact values can be realized in the feeding depends largely on the way in which the products are handled. Major Alvord, when Director of the Maryland Experiment Station, made a practical test to demonstrate the truth of the analysis of the different parts of the corn plant and showed conclusively that the same was correct. He divided the corn stalks into different sections. In one he had the ear, in another the top above the ear, in another the shuck and a short section of the stalk to which it was attached and in another the stalk below the ear. Each of these sections he fed to two steers in relatively the same proportions as their digestible nutrients called for and he got the same results from the feeding of the different parts. To secure, however, these results he had to grind the stalk and the hard parts to meal in order to make them palatable.. This showed that the digestible nutrients were there. The only question was how to secure their palatability in order to realize upon them. Shredding finely will largely meet this difficulty, but even this is not altogether sufficient. If when feeding shredded stover farmers would prepare the ration twelve or twenty-four hours beforehand and sprinkle the stover freely with water with a little salt in it and then cover the mass with old bags and let it heat and soften very little will be wasted when fed. We always fed it in this way and treated cut straw and hay in the same way. There is great economy in so feeding coarse fodder. Practically the stover so treated becomes a succulent feed like ensilage and is eaten as freely as ensilage. As to the point

that stover is as valuable as or nearly so as timothy hay, and which seems to be doubted, we based this also on the average analysis of the products and on experiments made at several stations in feeding both kinds of roughage. The digestible nutrients in one ton of stover and one ton of timothy hay are as follows:

	Corn stover lbs.	Timothy hay lbs.
Fiber	353.7	296.1
Fat	13.5	33.1
Protein	53.1	55.4
Nitrogen free extract	544.6	553.6
	964.6	938.2

This table we think fully justifies our statement. Timothy hay is the most over-rated long feed of any produced by American farmers. For our own feeding we would rather have good, sweet oat straw cut before the grain was over-ripe any day than the average timothy hay to be found on the market. If we grew timothy hay it would be solely for a sale crop. City horse keepers will always give more for it than it is worth to feed on the farm and we would let them have it and substitute corn stover, straw and mixed hay for feeding at home.

As to the lime question. We know that we are regarded as a sort of crank on this subject, but we are quite willing to accept the position. In our practical experience on the farm we have applied hundreds of tons of lime to our land and have done so at rates varying from two to five tons to the acre. We never saw that we had done any harm however heavy the application, but we constantly saw and reaped material benefit from its use. We are in the same position as a Pennsylvania farmer, a subscriber of ours, who wrote us sometime ago on the subject. He said that he had seen ten tons of lime applied per acre and that the land was in no way injured so far as any one could see. We believe now that we applied much more per acre when using two tons to the acre than gave profitable results. But at that time we only limed once in a seven-years rotation and if we could have kept the two tons in the upper strata of the soil through the seven years we believe that it would have been profitably used. Lime will, however, sink down quickly into the soil and long before the seven years had passed it was beyond the reach of most plants. If the same quantity had been used in three applications in the seven years we believe it would have been better. We think an application of one ton to the acre is little enough to give good results physically, mechanically and chemically and lime acts beneficially in all these three ways. If it does not cost the farmer more than $4.50 per ton on the farm it can be used profitably. This is the opinion of farmers in Maryland and Pennsylvania who have written us on the subject and they have had large experience in its use and it is an opinion in which we concur from our own practical experience. The handling and spreading of lime is not pleasant work and one need not hanker after the job but we have done it personally by a week at a time. It requires the exercise of common sense in the way it is done and then one need not be seriously inconvenienced. When we were using lime there was no machine made to spread it and therefore it had to be done by hand and for a reasonably heavy application this is still true, as few drills will put on more than 1,000 pounds to the acre. We always found that the best way to handle was to set it on the land in small lumps, say half a bushel in each just as it comes from the kiln and as soon after it has been drawn therefrom as haulage would permit. On each lump we sprinkled about half a bucket of water and let stand for an hour or so and then spread with a shovel. If water was not convenient to the field we would throw a few shovels full of damp soil on the heap and leave for a day or two and the whole would be found fallen. Spread always with the wind and thus keep the dust from falling on you and you need suffer little inconvenience. If the lime should be blown on to your skin wash with skimmed milk before using any water and the causticity will be killed.—Ed.

CORN BREEDING.

Editor Southern Planter:

I am glad to note that some of the Station workers are beginning to realize that the big and well-formed ear is not the only thing to be sought in the improvement of our corn crop. Professor Shoesmith, in The Planter for December, well says: "It has been found that the large, well-developed ear does not necessarily accompany the large yield of shelled corn per acre, but it is the yield per acre that we are seeking, and not necessarily ears of any particular type." I have for years been harping on that very point. I was at the corn show of the Maryland Corn Breeders' Association in Baltimore last week. There was an immense display of big ears, every one seeming to aim at getting the biggest ears. The judge went around and placed on certain samples different colored ribbons, deciding according to his score card. But if I had to take my seed corn out of the lot, I would not have given a toss of a penny between the ears that bore the blue ribbon and those that failed to get any award. In fact, the judge could not, for the life of him, tell whether the blue ribbon sample would, when used for seed, make more corn per acre than the samples he passed over.

These exhibitions of ears of corn show that score card breeding has improved the type of ears; only this and nothing more, and in what way the improvement in the size and shape of ears has advanced the product of corn I do not believe that any of the score card breeders can tell.

If we are to have corn shows of value, we must show the whole thing. We must bring the corn plant, root and top and ears, and then let the judges study the plants and not only one feature of them. At this same corn show the Maryland Experiment Station had an exhibit of corn varieties. Among these there were samples of Cocke's Prolific, a corn we grew in North Carolina for years. Few took any notice of it because the ears were small in comparison with those of the Leaming and others of the big eared class. And yet, I would be willing to guarantee that I could make many bushels more per acre from it than from the Leaming. When corn shows show the whole plant and its product and each exhibit is accompanied with a statement of the method of planting and cultivation and the yield per acre, we will be advanc-

ing somewhat. But breeding for pretty ears alone will never sensibly increase the corn crop, and it is about time that this sort of corn-show foolishness was stopped, and some effort made to introduce real corn breeding. One thing at the show that did not attract as much attention as it should was the germination text-box that the Maryland Experiment Station showed. I noticed that nearly all the corn exhibited was rather immature, or at least had a good deal of moisture still in it, and this late season will require more attention to the germinating quality of the grain than usual. No one who has ever tested seed corn or other seed carefully will understand the great variation there may be in the vitality of different ears of corn. The man who is careless in this matter may have a great deal of re-planting to do, while his neighbor, who pays attention to the getting of the highest germinating quality in his seed corn, will have a perfect stand. We need in the first place to breed the plant well, and to establish a heredity of productiveness, and then to be sure that we have cured the seed corn so as to retain the strongest vitality.

Lawyers and Farmers.

What Mr. Patteson says about the respective dignity and profit of the so-called learned professions and the profession of agriculture reminds me of the time ten years ago when I was called upon to undertake the improvement of the great farm of the Miller School of Albemarle. I objected to the salary offered and the chairman of the Board, in a surprised sort of way, said: "Why, I know lots of lawyers in Charlottesville who do not make that much." I told him they would doubtless make still less if placed in charge of that farm. About thirty years ago, the farmers of Maryland wanted to get the Maryland Agricultural College into its legitimate work, for it had been doing nothing of the sort, but had become a sort of refuge for broken down preachers and retired naval officers, and they nominated me for the presidency. The politicians had their candidate, and finally succeeded in electing him by the casting vote of the then Commissioner of Agriculture, Mr. Loring. During the series of meetings in which there was a tie vote, one of the members urged my election because I had a reputation as a practical farmer. "What do we want with a farmer as President of the College?" said the Governor, the ex-officio Chairman, "I can hire all the farmers I want for $20 a month." "Why, then, do we have an Agricultural College if we are to teach the boys that a farmer is only worth $20 a month," retorted the other gentleman. This low idea of the importance of the profession of agriculture did more in the early history of the colleges in all the States than anything else to belittle the work. But the ideas of the public in regard to the dignity and importance of the profession of farming have been much enlightened of late years, and it has been mainly through the work of the Experiment Stations which have given to the colleges the matter to teach. The Agricultural College of to-day is the child of the Experiment Stations. The general public, too, has come to understand that the colleges are not merely training schools for farm hands, but are real technical colleges, whose degrees carry as much weight among scientific men as those of any other class.

But I do not agree with Mr. Patteson that the University

of Virginia should teach agriculture. The effort in that line years ago on the Miller foundation was not encouraging. In fact, as a mere University study, agriculture has seldom been well taught. Far better concentrate on the Virginia Polytechnic Institute. The University is a great institution, with a noble history, but it is not big enough to teach agriculture as it is demanded at this present day. The Miller Fund in the University is doing more good as a Department of Biology than it ever could do in agriculture.

Tomatoes Under Glass.

The Editor is perfectly right in telling Mr. Cox, of Norfolk county, that tomatoes cannot be grown successfully in a cold pit. They might be wintered over in such a structure and be considerably earlier in late spring than the outside crop, but to ripen tomatoes during the winter requires artificial heat other than the mere sun heat under glass. The temperature at night should never be under 60 degrees and a good deal higher in daytime, and while the unheated structure might get as warm as needed when the sun shone, it would be entirely too cold in dark weather and at night. In Eastern Virginia the forcing of tomatoes in greenhouses can be done more cheaply than in the North, owing to the abounding sunshine in winter and the absence of the long, dark spells common on the Northern Atlantic coast. For this reason, less fuel will be needed. But the man who undertakes tomato forcing in winter in any make-shift house will find that his experience has cost him a good deal. In fact, winter forcing under glass calls for a high degree of skill on the part of the gardener. But in the South Atlantic coast country the tendency is in that direction. The use of steam in the cloth-covered lettuce frames in North Carolina is one step towards real winter work. Horticultural work is rapidly cut up into specialties, and one man does not attempt to grow everything. I met only last week a man who has five acres covered with glass in heated greenhouses, and his main business is the production of young plants for other gardeners to set. He told me that he sowed last season nine bushels of pepper seed alone and cabbage and tomato and other seed by the cartload.

In one large establishment near Philadelphia there are acres of glass, and all used for the production of palms and ferns.

In New England there are numerous places where the sole business is the production of cucumbers in winter, and these, as well as tomatoes, can be more economically grown in the upper South. But the man must know how and must have a modern equipment for the business.

Corn on High Land.

The Editor advises "Subscriber" right in regard to corn for high land. I met a large farmer a few days ago who told me that he had planted the finest ears of corn he ever saw, and was not satisfied with the yield he got. From his description of the corn, I found that he planted the big-eared Gourd-seed or horse-tooth corn—a type only suited to moist lowland and very rich soil, while his land was sandy upland.

A farmer, going to one of the corn shows and selecting the big ears for seed, would probably be disappointed in the yield, if he planted the seed on ordinary dry upland. I would advise "Subscriber" to get the best corn grown on upland that he can find in his neighborhood and not to send off and get some he will have to acclimate. Then breed it for yourself.

Nut Grass.

The most efficient exterminator of nut grass is a flock of geese kept on it all the season to prevent its seeding and to keep the tops nipped off continually. There are a hundred plants of nut grass that come from seed to every one that is produced from the tubers. If the tops are continually nipped off, as the geese will nip them, the plant will give up the effort and the hogs can finish the roots.   W. F. MASSEY.

CROP ROTATION—LIME—FARM HORSES—TIMBER
Editor Southern Planter:

In the December issue of your most valuable Journal Mr. Hicks criticizes the crop rotation suggested in a previous issue by Mr. Coleman and asks for further discussion of the subject. At Bullfield a four-field rotation was begun this year, and is given below, together with the rotations used by Mr. Coleman and Mr. Hicks:

	FIELD I.	FIELD II.	FIELD III.	FIELD IV.
Coleman.	Oats and Vetch	Cow Peas and Crimson Clover	Crimson Clover for Corn	
Hicks.	Crimson Clover for Corn	Peas followed by Oats	Oats followed by Crimson Clover	
Bullfield.	Corn with Crimson Clover	Crimson Clover followed by Oats	Oats Harvest	Red and Alsike Clover

At Bullfield the crimson clover is seeded between the corn rows with a combination weeder and seeder. The red and alsike clovers are seeded with the oats, together with 300 pounds of phosphate and 100 pounds of bone, followed later by a top dressing of stable manure at the rate of three loads per acre. This year the seeder arrived too late for using it in the corn and the seed was scattered on the ground before rains. Where the crimson clover fails, or where the seed could not be put in on time, the corn stubble is disked and seeded to thirty pounds of vetch, one-half bushel of oats, and one-quarter bushel of wheat, together with 300 pounds of phosphate. The vetch is intended for hay. The corn is cultivated flat with riding disk cultivators and the crimson clover might also be harvested for hay if we could get rid of the corn stubble.

This rotation permits of clean summer fallowing the second year (between the crimson clover and the oat crops), or green fallowing by sowing cow peas or cow peas with millet for hay, if other work permits ploughing early enough.

The rotation used by Mr. Hicks is perhaps subject to the criticism that it leaves the corn stubble land bare all winter, which is undesirable.

The most difficult part about liming the land seems to be the getting of the lime at a reasonable price. Agricultural lime is offered by one kiln advertising in the October issue of the Southern Planter at $1.50 per ton,

In car lots, and farmers living on its line of railroad should readily avail themselves of the offer. Some kilns seem to have entered into a deal to furnish all their agricultural lime to fertilizer firms at $2 per ton, or less, and these same kilns ask farmers $3 per ton—rather steep when you bear in mind that shipments in either case are made directly from the kiln in car lots. Where the freight is from $1 to $1.50 per ton, the lime would cost from $4 to $4.50 per ton, which is more than farmers can afford to pay.

Farmers should bear in mind that other fertilizers should never be mixed with lime nor spread at the same time. Dealers in fertilizers pretending to sell prepared lime as fertilizer are taking advantage of the ignorance of their customers.

Thoroughbreds and thoroughbred-scrub mixtures are entirely too light for ordinary farm work. It is well that more Percheron stallions are going into service to give us a heavier stock. Trotters and running horses are well enough for racing stables, but will not do for the average farm. It doe not cost more to raise a Percheron grade colt from an ordinary farm mare than it does to raise a little runt, and the former will usually fetch $50 more than the latter.

Admitting that Percheron and Shire grades are profitable to raise, it does not follow that they are the best all-round farm horses. They are gentle and faithful workers, but bulky, and their gait is not suited to farm work. The best all-round farm horse is undoubtedly the German coach, sixteen to seventeen hands high, weighing from thirteen to fifteen hundred pounds. They are clean of limb, graceful, and quick of action. They are neither trotters, runners nor drafters, but if you have a shapely mare to breed from, a pair of well matched high-steppers will fetch big money. And for all-round farm work they have no equal. Still, until they are more generally introduced and appreciated, we welcome the Percherons, Shires, etc., to give us a heavier stock that will pull a big load and will bring good prices when sold.

How many horses should be kept on the farm for each man at work—speaking of the farmer doing his own work with the aid of his boys?

Following the plow behind a pair of little runts is not doing a day's work. The man can just as readily handle three or four large horses hitched to the gang-plow and much of the machinery requires really more than two horses. A farm with three willing men should probably have eight or nine horses, and perhaps a few more, if half of them are brood mares.

On the other hand, the keeping of more horses than can profitably be worked is an expensive luxury, as is also the keeping and feeding of any span of horses that is not large and strong enough to do a good day's work. Any good farmer's time is too valuable to waste it behind a team of runts.

Virginia land will grow to trees without planting any. Sure! And the land will grow up to grass without seeding. But the trees will likely be field pines, dogwood, and what not and the grass, will be broom straw. Neither is very profitable.

If your timber lands average less than $3 per acre per year clear profit, it might pay to read how forests are farmed in Saxony. What Virginia farmer is getting $3 per year year in and year out, net profit, from his 100 acre lot of timber? And yet, we know that a clean even stand of yellow pine, fifty years old, may fetch $300 per acre if conveniently located as to transportation. A 100 acre lot, divided into fifty fields, will allow of harvesting two acres of trees fifty years old every year.　　　　N.

A NEW BREED—DUROC HOGS AT V. P. I.,
BLACKSBURG, VIRGINIA.

Editor Southern Planter:

The red breed of swine, which has grown so rapidly popular in the South, has been under consideration for some time for class and experimental work at the Agricultural College of the Virginia Polytechnic Institute. The securing of specimens of this breed was perhaps reached at an earlier date than it otherwise would have been by two very valuable donations. The first of these consisted of two very excellent last spring's gilts, donated by Mr. Leslie D. Kline, of Vaucluse, Va., from his famous herd, to which he has brought within the last year two carloads of splendidly bred Durocs from the best herds of the Central West. The other donation also comes from an excellent herd—that of Mr. Walter M. Carroll, of Lynchburg, who has also drawn on the very best show and breeding herds of the United States for his leading Duroc families, Mr. Carroll's donation is that of a young herd boar of magnificent proportions, an almost ideal specimen of the breed and not related to the two fine gilts donated by Mr. Kline.

To make complete and more effective the work with the Duroc breed, the Agricultural Department has made purchase of five other excellent females representing different and leading strains of the breed. These females have all been bred this fall, which gives promise of the starting of a nice young herd in the spring. The offspring from this breeding will doubtless supply some surplus that may be experimented with during the summer and fall, and finally land as good prospective breeders in the Annual Reduction Sale of V. P. I. next Thanksgiving, when farmers will again have the opportunity of purchasing offspring of the herds of this Institution at their own prices.

WALTER J. QUICK,
Dean and Professor of Animal Husbandry,
Virginia Polytechnic Institute.

James City Co., Va., Dec. 14, 1907.

I have been a constant reader of the Southern Planter as long as I have been in the State and on the farm—about twenty years, now—and would not want to be without it, as I think it the best of the many farm papers I read, the best, sure, for our section.　　G. HELM.

Pulaski Co., Va., Dec. 17, 1907.

The Southern Planter is the most excellent Journal of its kind with which I am familiar, and I would not be without it.　　MRS. J. LAREW.

Trucking, Garden and Orchard.

WORK FOR THE MONTH.

It is too early to think of planting anything this month except in the far South, where the earliest spring salads may be seeded and English peas be sown. Towards the end of the month English peas are sometimes sown in Eastern North Carolina and Tidewater Virginia, but the weather should be very mild if this is done, and the land be in a fine condition. We doubt much whether anything is gained by planting so early. It is true that English peas will, if planted deeply, take no harm waiting in the ground for it to warm up so a to cause them to germinate, but they are almost sure to be checked later by a cold spell.

The work of preparing compost heaps for use upon the land to be planted in spring crops should have attention. These should be made up of manure and vegetable refuse matter of all kinds, mixed thoroughly together and of rich soil from the woods. With these should be mixed acid phosphate and muriate of potash liberally. All vegetables are great consumers of these mineral plant foods and take time to become avalable. Mixed in the compost heaps, they will be more effective than if applied to the land at planting time. These compost heaps should be turned over once or twice before being gotten out on the land and the plant food will then be in good available condition when applied. Use the phosphate and potash at a rate sufficiently heavy to give from 500 to 700 pounds of phosphate to the acre and from 100 to 200 pounds to the acre of the potash.

Plough and break the land to be planted whenever the soil is dry and will work freely without sticking to the plow. Do not plough wet land, or you will never be able to make a satisfactory seed-bed. After ploughing, get the compost on the land and commence to work it in. Harrow and work frequently and thus ensure the soil being thoroughly broken and the compost completely mixed throughout the whole depth of the soil.

The work of pruning and cleaning up the orchard, vineyard and small fruit plantations should have attention so that this work may be out of the way when the time for planting crops is at hand. Cut out all dead and interfering branches in the fruit trees, and open out the head. Shorten back all new canes of raspberries and blackberries and cut out the old canes. It is yet too early to prune grape vines. Next month is better.

APPLE GROWING IN VIRGINIA.

Extract from Address Delivered by Prof. J. S. Phillips, State Entomologist, Before the American Pomological Society, at the Jamestown Exposition Meeting, September, 1907.

(Continued from December issue.)

The bitter rot of the apple was, at one time, considered a very serious enemy also. While the general recommendation to spray with Bordeaux mixture has been made over and over again in the State and followed out to some extent, it remained for the demonstration by Mr. W. M. Scott to bring this matter prominently before the Virginia growers. This work in the orchard of Mr. Goodwin at Afton, Virginia, proved successful, and growers in this section are generally adopting the methods.

The development, especially in the apple industry, is now at its high-water mark, the older growers being extremely enthusiastic as to the future of this industry. I could name fifteen or twenty large commercial orchard companies that have been organized in the State during the past two years. Much of this work, too, is being conducted wisely, taking its initiative from the conditions obtaining in the orchards in the immediate vicinity. The movement extends over the entire orchard belt of the State, from Eastern Piedmont almost to the farthest confines in the West. In Patrick county alone the companies recently organized reach an aggregate capital of $100,000 and their plantings will amount to some 60,000 to 75,000 trees.

In point of production of apples, the Valley section is now taking the lead. Though the statistics gathered by the Experiment Station for 1903 cannot be considered as representing the entire crop, they are the best and most reliable we have and serve to indicate to some extent the counties from which the largest shipments were made. In 1903, Frederick county led with 76,308 barrels, followed by Augusta with 40,957, and, in the Southwest, Wythe county was not far in the rear with 25,000, and Roanoke 23,953.

Though Frederick led Augusta county in 1903, she must look well to her laurels, for in no part of the State do I consider the outlook brighter than in Augusta. The number of apple trees in Augusta would now likely reach 500,000, and her peaches from 300,000 to 400,000. She has also quite a good inspection force, which is helping greatly in the fight against San Jose scale and peach yellows—a fight which is absolutely necessary if peach growing is to develop.

Some of the very best growers refuse absolutely to sell to dealers, preferring rather to superintend the picking, packing and marketing of their own fruits. For various reasons, this should be more satisfactory than selling the apples on the trees and should build up a reputation for the individual grower, which is worth much as stock in trade.

The success of this method is proven by the fact that Mr. Miller, of Rappahannock county, with some 12,000 to 13,000 trees, at times has received as high as $9.75 per barrel for his Pippins, and $5 to $7 for his best Winesaps and York Imperials. Other growers report similar success.

The tendency of many orchards in the State is to bear one crop in two years, but some growers are attempting to handle their orchards in such a way as to produce fair crops every year instead. Mr. John L. Wissler, of the Strathmore Orchard Company, in Shenandoah county, has a large orchard of York Imperials, which bore their first

crop when eight years old, averaging one-half barrel per
tree. This yield increased annually to an average of
three and one-half barrels the twelfth year—1906—with
but one off-year during the five-year period. One of his
small orchards of Ben Davis bore one-sixth of a barrel
at five years old and increased annually to an average of
three barrels per tree at thirteen years of age, without a
single off-year.

If our growers can, by mastery of the conditions, thorough and judicious cultivation, pruning, spraying, fertiliz-
ing, etc., succeed in producing a crop each year, an important epoch in apple growing will have been reached.
Some of the important considerations are to prevent over
bearing and to supply the trees with sufficient nourishment
when laden with fruit to enable them not only to mature
the crop of fruit, but to mature a sufficient number of fruit
buds to produce a crop the following year, and to limit
cultivation during the off-year.

Occupying, as she does, almost the Southern limit for
the successful growth of winter apples, and thus being
near the Southern markets, Virginia has the advantage of
nearness to shipping points for export, and within a few
hours of Philadelphia, New York and other Northern
cities. This happy location, with her ideal soil and climatic conditions, railroad facilities, etc., give her a commanding position in the apple industry. She also occu-
pies about the Northern limit for the successful growth
of very late peaches, among them the Bilyeu, Heath Cling,
Salway, Smock, etc. The commanding position she has
already obtained in the markets of the world for these
fruits help to give her a prominence and outlook for the
future of this commercial industry hardly equalled by any
other State in the Union.

TIDEWATER VIRGINIA TRUCK CROP EXPERIMENT STATION.

Editor Southern Planter:

Your readers will undoubtedly be interested in the fact
that through the concerted efforts of the truck growers
in the vicinity of Norfolk, Virginia, and the State Board
of Agriculture, there has been established, just outside
the city of Norfolk, in Princess Anne county, an Experiment Station devoted exclusively to the interests of truck
growing. This Station has been placed under the immediate charge of Professor T. C. Johnson, formerly of Cor-
nell and of the West Virginia University. The Station is
located upon characteristic trucking soil of the region and
embraces some fifty-eight acres, which will be improved
and devoted to the cultivation of various truck crops, and
the solution of the many problems involved in the fertilization, harvesting, marketing and improvement of such
crops. Seven thousand five hundred dollars ($7,500) have
been set aide by the Southern Produce Company for the
purpose of equipping this tract with suitable buildings for
conducting the work. The State Board of Agriculture
devotes $5,000 of its funds to the maintenance of the
work, and the Department of Agriculture at Washington,
and the State Experiment Station at Blacksburg, Virginia,
both cooperate with above named organizations in carrying on the work. While no experimental work has yet
been inaugurated, the ground is being improved and prepared for the work of actual experimentation. It is

hoped that as the spring opens areas will be available
for extensive fertilizer and variety tests, as well as the
beginning of some systematic breeding work with standard vegetables. This is a notable undertaking in this
respect that it is the first experiment Station to be organized in the United States exclusively devoted to the
interests of truck growers of any locality. The organization is to be congratulated on having secured the ser-
vices of a careful, conservative and well-trained man in
the person of Professor Johnson, and all possible success
is hoped for the undertaking. It is a new field of work
and will of course present innumerable problems, a few
only of which can be taken up and solved at once. It
will be necessary to devote years of careful study and
research to this industry which has sprung up and grown
to such gigantic proportions in comparatively few years;
that is, the many problems peculiar to itself which have
never been touched upon by the regular experiment station workers of the country, and it is fortunate that this
station has been established in a region so preeminently
devoted to trucking as is the territory in the neighborhood of Norfolk and Portsmouth, Virginia.

Very truly yours,
L. C. Corbett, Horticulturist.
Department of Agriculture (Bureau of Plant Industry),
Washington, D. C.

We are glad to know that this station is now established and put in charge of a competent and experienced,
scientific man. We shall look to it to give much help to
our truck growers and place our columns at the service
of the Director for communicating any matter which he
may think of interest to the truckers.—Ed.

THE VIRGINIA STATE HORTICULTURAL SOCIETY.

The society held a most successful meeting at Staunton
on the 4th and 5th of December. The meetings were
presided over by the Hon. G. E. Murrell, the President.
The attendance was a record one and great attention was
given to the various addresses and papers which were
delivered and read and the subjects were fully discussed
by the members. Amongst the resolutions adopted was
one asking that an appropriation of $5,000 be made by
the Legislature of Virginia to extend and aid the work
of the society and a committe was appointed to press
this on the attention of the Legislature. The society is
doing a great work for the advancement of the fruit industry in the State and ought to have the support of the
State. It was also decided to organize an Apple Packer's
Association for Piedmont Virginia to be framed after the
very successful one which handles the Oregon apples. Of
this organization, Dr. J. R. Guerrant, of Calloway, Va., was
made President; R. E. Wayland, of Crozet, Secretary, and
Walter Whately, of Crozet, Va., Treasurer. In connection
with the meeting there was held the finest exhibit of
Virginia apples ever got together at one time. These
were shown in comparison with the finest apples got from
Oregon, Colorado and Western States and they did not
suffer from the comparison. Prizes were keenly con-
tested for and Prof. Gould and Messrs. J. B. Watkins and
W. T. Hood and the other members of the committee of
awards had a long, hard task in awarding the same. Dr.
Guerrant won the beautiful silver challenge loving cup

offered by Dr. J. B. Emerson for the best display of apples. He took prizes on nearly every entry he made. The officers of the Society were re-elected with one or two minor changes of Vice-Presidents. The Hon. G. E. Murrell, President; Walter Whately, Secretary and Treasurer, and Prof. H. L. Price, Recording Secretary. We congratulate the society on the success of the meeting at which more new members were elected than at any previous gathering.

THE SCUPPERNONG GRAPE.

Editor Southern Planter:

The States of Virginia, North Carolina and South Carolina have a valuable grape in the Scuppernong.

It reaches its greatest perfection in the counties bordering the Atlantic, and the Sounds of Albemarle and Pamlico.

It has been tried with indifferent success in many other States. The vine grows quickly, is long-lived, hardy and vigorous, and almost immune from disease.

It is the largest domestic grape known, often measuring two and a half to three inches in circumference. When the fruit is ripening its fragrance fills the air with a delicious aroma. The skin is thick and tough, but the fruit soft and juicy with a luscious flavor peculiarly its own. It is extremely popular in the South for the table, and as a wine grape the demand far exceeds the spply.

Commercially, this grape could be made a most valuable asset in the section indicated, but as yet very little attention has been given to it as a means of revenue. With care and cultivation a thrifty vine will produce more than double the amount of fruit and wine per acre of any grape in the world. The vines commence to bear the second year. It is estimated from vines five years old, an income of from $200 to $500 per acre can be secured,

while more than double that amount can be depended on in ten or twelve years.

In fifteen years an acre should yield an income of from $1,000 to $1,500. A well-cared for vineyard has been known to yield over a thousands bushels to the acre in a good season.

The market price this year has been from $1.75 to $2.00 per bushel of sixty pounds. Under present conditions the possibilities are immense. It is a crop that never fails, and the cost of cultivation, after the first year,

compared with the labor expended on cotton, tobacco, peanuts, etc., is trifling. One hundred and ten vines to

the acre is enough. Eac h vine should average eight to ten bushels.

Good grape growing lands can be bought to-day in Eastern North Carolina for $8 to $12 per acre, and we have shown that in fifteen years a ten-acre farm should yield an income of from $10,000 to $15,000 per year.

The fruit makes a clear, light wine of very delicate flavor, and, as before stated, the demand so far exceeds the supply, that the product of a vineyard is engaged in advance from year to year.

Before planting the ground must be well plowed and fertilized. Posts placed at intervals of 10 or 12 feet, 7 feet high, with wire or slats overhead make the most approved arbor. No trimming is done to the vines, and as the fruit ripens it is quickly gathered by shaking it into sheets or canvas placed beneath.

Harking back to 1586 we read in the report made to Sir Walter Raleigh by Captain Amadas upon his return to England from Roanoke Island, North Carolina, the following reference to grapes: "Which being performed (i. e. possesion taken) according to the ceremonies used in such enterprises, we viewed the land about us, being very sandy and low toward the water side, but so full of grapes as the very beating and surge of the sea overflowed them that I think in all the world the like abundance is not to be found, and myself having seen those parts of Europe that most abound, find such difference as were incredible to be written."

The larger vine shown in the illustration is believed to be over 300 years old. It is still growing, hearty and vigorous, on Roanoke Island, N. C., not far from the original landing place of Captain Amadas and his colonists, and where for the first time the flag of old England was unfurled to the breezes of the new World.

The smaller vine is but four years old; it extends a distance of over 30 feet from end to end, and at least 10 feet of the vine to the left does not show in the picture. It yielded well the past season, and would have done better had it been trailed on an overhead arbor, instead of on an upright one. It shows the rapid growth of this species. It is located on Carter's Creek, Lancaster County, Virginia, not far from the Rappahannock river.

Lancaster Co., Va.   A. D. DART.

Live Stock and Dairy.

SWINE HUSBANDRY IN THE SOUTH; NECESSITY FOR SUCCESSIVE GRAZING CROPS.

The Hog Omnivorous and Ubiquitous.

Editor Southern Planter:

An Ohio farmer who is extensively engaged in raising hogs for market remarked recently that "Among the important reasons why hogs are profitable is the comparatively limited area in which they can be economically produced, and subsisting on corn they are not a profitable proposition except within the limits of the corn belt,' so-called. To the above declaration I beg to enter both a demurrer and a plea, the former because his statements are not in harmony with the laws governing the nature of the hog and the latter, because they misrepresent existing facts. In Europe, Canada, many parts of the Northwest and in the South hogs are raised profitably without corn. Corn has its place and a very important place in hog feeding, but there are substitutes and it is now an established fact, amply proven by careful experiments, that corn alone does not furnish satisfactory nutrients for the hog. It must be balanced with nitrogenous compounds and roughages must be furnished in the form of pasturage in summer and stored crops in winter to maintain the health, vigor and prolificacy of the animals. There is not a State in this Union where pork cannot be economically produced. Prof. Cottrell, of the Colorado Experiment Station, has recently issued a statement showing that hogs are being produced very profitably in that State entirely without the use of corn. Barley, rye, cow peas, clover, alfalfa and wheat products, with digester tankage, will put the balance sheet right without an appeal to the corn belt. In one instance, a Mr. Hart, near Denver, put 122 pigs, twelve weeks old, on eight acres of alfalfa pasture. No grain was fed. The pigs were sold in the fall for $1,100. They were worth $250 when turned on the alfalfa, giving $850 in profit from the eight acres.

Virginia has become a great fruit producing State and many of the orchardists are finding that hogs go well with the orchard, the crops that are raised in them, and the abundance of shade.

Virginia and other sections of the South have superior advantages for dairy husbandry and the demand for high grade dairy products was never greater. Hog raising fits in admirably with almost any scheme of dairy farming and if a prize were offered for the best and most economical production of pork, some dairy farmer would be sure of the reward. Skim milk is unquestionably the best possible adjunct to successful pig raising. If skim milk cannot be had digester tankage will prove a close second. The Michigan Experiment Station, as well as many others, including the Virginia Station, secured excellent results with tankage, when fed in the proportion of from one-eighth to one-tenth of the concentrated diet. I have found both digester tankage and linseed meal a valuable ration in winter feeding.

The writer has received numerous letters in regard to cottonseed meal as a protein substitute for skim milk. Theoretically, from the standpoint of digestible nutrients,

it should be a valuable feed for hogs, but it has a toxic effect on swine which usually proves fatal, unless fed in a very restricted way and should not be recommended to the inexperienced feeder.

The South as a Field for Swine Husbandry.

No section has more advantages and fewer disadvantages to offer the swine breeder to-day than the South. Long growing seasons, an ideal climate, plenty of pure water, numerous wild and cultivated foods and the comparative freedom of the section from disease, together with an unsurpassed home market, make the South the most favored area on earth for the production of pig products. Prof. S. M. Tracy, of the U. S. Department of Agriculture, in Bulletin No. 100 says: "The Southern States can produce corn almost if not quite as cheaply as the most favored regions of Illinois and Missouri, while the much greater variety of food crops, the more nearly continuous grazing and the consequent greater immunity from disease give special advantages for profitable pork raising which do not exist elsewhere."

In 1900 fully 80 per cent. of the pork consumed in the South was shipped into this section from the great packing houses of the Middle-West. Millions of dollars are sent out of this section annually for meat that could have been produced at considerably less cost at home. Recent statistics show, however, that during the last few years an increased interest has been developed throughout the South in breeding and raising hogs. The animated razorback plow is no longer seen and many fine herds of pure-bred hogs are maintained in every Southern State. It has been found that the hog is the real mortgage-lifter among the domestic animals and by putting money into the purse of his owner he has found a short road to public favor. But while a keener interest is being manifested in swine husbandry throughout the South, old methods are being largely adhered to, with attendant meagre results in many cases, while a change of methods would mean a better condition for the hogs themselves with

A DUROC-JERSEY SOW.

larger profits for their owners. It has been estimated that from one to two million additional hogs could be raised in each Southern State each year at a profit to those engaged in the business and with possibilities for unlimited soil improvement, by intelligent management.

Selecting the Foundation Herd.

In the limited scope of this paper it is impossible to go into the question of breeds or to more than touch upon the selection of the foundation herd. Suffice it to state that too much care cannot be taken in the selection of the breeding stock. For many reasons I prefer a purebred herd, even for raising hogs for market. The offspring will be more uniform and will command higher prices and each mating will not in turn present a Chinese puzzle as to what the issue will be. The scrub should be sent to the realm of shade with the wooden plow, grain cradle and spinning wheel. At the present price of land, labor and feed, it is nothing less than an indictment against a farmer's business sagacity to persist in breeding mongrels. At all events, the males used in the herd should be pure-breds and to get pure-bred males we must have pure-bred herds. The hogs selected should possess a store of inherited vitality and vigor. There must be no congenital tendencies to constitutional weakness or the venture will be foredoomed to failure. The animal must convert a large amount of material into marketable products, in a very short period of time and any weakness whatever, will result in a failure to carry to profitable consummation its purpose in life.

In selecting the herd, then, regard must be had to those types which meet utility demands, and a system of management and feeding must be practiced which will insure prolificacy, the production of strong healthy pigs to begin with, which will develop a good frame and internal organs, so that when the time comes for fattening we will have an animal with strong powers of digestion and assimilation and capable of withstanding heavy forced feeding and arrive at the slaughter-house without having developed any form of constitutional weakness.

Arrangement of Lots and Hog-houses.

Every farmer who attempts to raise hogs should have a number of lots fenced with pig-proof fence and convenient to his hog barn or houses. A good plan is to have a tract of land with a roadway extending along one side of it, or through it, with lots on both sides. These lots should be as near one size as possible and the gates opening into them should be the same width as the road, and made to swing across it. This will facilitate matters when it is desired to move the hogs from one lot to another. These lots should be seeded in different crops in order to furnish continuous grazing for the hogs during the greater part of the year. With mill feed at $1.40 per cwt. and corn at $3.00 to $3.50 per bbl. it is quite possible to come out at the little end of the horn in selling hogs at $6.00 to $6.50 gross. With the proper succession of grazing crops and supplementing with the concentrates in order to get a balanced ration in some instances, it is possible to make a handsome profit at these prices, for both the grain and the marketable hogs.

Permanent Pasture.

Lot number one should be seeded in grass for a permanent pasture; either blue grass or, a mixture of blue grass and white clover, or in some sections orchard grass and in still other sections—farther south—Bermuda grass.

It is well to build the hog-houses on this lot. They should not be expensive, but should be dry, well ventilated and admit the sunshine, comparatively warm in winter and cool in summer and free from cold draughts and should be so arranged as to be easily cleaned. The portable hog-houses are rapidly coming into favor and justly so. In

A DUROC-JERSEY BOAR.

building a hog-house of any size nothing will pay better than an investment in doors and window glass. Disinfectants are alright, but can never be substituted for cleanliness and sunshine. Microbes that prove the most fruitful source of disease are but the foul brood of darkness, dampness and dirt. These three "d's" spell death to pigs. Biologists have shown that sunlight destroys disease germs.

Dwarf Essex Rape.

Lot number two should be seeded in Dwarf Essex rape as early in the spring as possible; in Virginia by the 20th of April. The rape will do to pasture in from four to six weeks, as it is quick growing and thrives wherever corn is a dependable crop and produces an enormous amount of green, rich forage that is relished by both hogs and sheep. Rape can be planted in corn at the last cultivation of the latter and will then make an excellent fall pasture. At the Wisconsin Station where much attention has been given to this crop, it was demonstrated that pigs thrive better on rape than clover, grain being fed in both cases. Several of the experiment stations found it possible to keep brood sows in good condition on Dwarf Essex rape with very little grain. The writer has used rape with the most satisfactory results and pastured it continually this year from June 20th till December 15th.

Sorghum.

Lot number three should be planted in early amber sorghum about the last of April or the first of May. It should be cut in the fall and shocked near the winter quarters and fed to the hogs when no other succulent food is available. For fattening hogs, or for sows that are suckling pigs, sorghum is most valuable. A good plan is to mix some sorghum with the rape seed and sow the two broadcast, and harrow them in. This furnishes one of the best grazing crops we have tried.

Soy Beans, Cow Peas and Corn.

Lot number four may be planted in soy beans, or cow

peas, or better still in corn and soy beans, as soon as the ground is warm enough—say the first of May, in Virginia. The corn and soy beans can be mixed and drilled with the corn planter. At the last cultivation, cow peas should be planted between the rows and the whole crop "hogged" off late in the fall. This combination will furnish a splendid balance ration for the hogs and they can be finished for market on it without additional grain. At the present price of farm labor, this will pay better than harvesting, husking, hauling and carrying the crop to the hogs, besides saving hauling the manure out again. In this system of successive grazing crops there is no need of a $125 manure spreader. To prevent waste of corn, both grown hogs and pigs should be turned on this lot. The pigs will eat the shattered grains which the hogs leave.

Artichokes.

Lot number five should be planted in Jerusalem artichokes. No crop will give larger returns for land and labor than artichokes. Some of the successful Western herders fit their hogs for the fairs on artichokes alone. The hogs can be turned on them during the late summer, fall and early winter months.

Alfalfa.

Lot number six can be seeded in alfalfa early in the spring, in order to get a good foot-hold before the weeds come, or in August, after they have germinated and been killed by successive harrowings. Probably the spring seeding is the better plan in this section. In the middle eastern and southern sections early fall seeding is to be preferred. The ground should be thoroughly prepared, given an application of stable manure, commercial fertilizer, and lime, if the soil is acid, and unless the reader is familiar with the methods of preparing the soil and seeding alfalfa he should consult the back numbers of the Southern Planter, write to his experiment station, or to the U. S. Department of Agriculture. The alfalfa will furnish pasture for several years if properly handled, and can be grazed off four or five times during each season. It is one of the earliest as well as one of the latest crops and will well repay any one for the trouble in growing it.

Crimson Clover, Rye, Wheat and Oats.

Lot number seven should be seeded in crimson clover and a mixture of rye, winter wheat and winter oats, or either of these cereals. This may be pastured during the fall and winter and in the spring and a crop of grain may then be raised and "hogged" off.

Peanuts.

Further south and in many parts of Virginia, Spanish peanuts have proven a profitable crop for hogs and even in northern Virginia they can be used in rotation with other crops and made to pay. They should be planted at about the same time as corn.

Chufas.

Chufas do well in the sandy soil of the South and have proven a splendid crop for hogs.

Sugar Beets and Mangel, and Cooking Foods.

Both sugar beets and mangel wurzles will be found valuable for winter feeding. The sugar beets are probably the better, but it will pay to raise some of both if the soil conditions wil admit of it. We do not recommend cooking them, in fact, we believe it a waste of time to cook any food for hogs excepting Irish potatoes and possibly turnips and pumpkins. Cooking, it is believed, has the effect of

reducing the digestibility of the protein, the most expensive constituent in all feeding stuffs.

Cassava.

Cassava has given good results in the southern coast region. It is rich in food elements which belong to the fat-forming group and when fed in connection with middlings, cow peas or peanuts, it furnishes an unexcelled ration for growing or fattening hogs.

Clover.

Lot number eight should be seeded in a mixture of red, alsike and sapling clovers. The best time to seed this is about the first of August and the ground should be carefully prepared, given an application of acid phosphate at the time of seeding. With "pigs in clover" there is little use to worry about the pigs or the pocketbook.

Vetches.

Winter oats or rye and hairy vetch make a splendid pasture and this mixture may be seeded on any of the lots during the late summer or early fall, after the hogs have finished with the spring crops seeded thereon. It would be possible to follow rape, sorghum or peanuts with winter oats or rye and vetches and thereby obtain a superior winter and spring pasture.

Hogs should be fed some grain while grazing these crops, excepting the cereal and some of the leguminous crops named above.

Possibilities of Grazing Crops.

By a succession of grazing crops, as outlined above, it is possible to fit hogs for market at from two-fifths to three-fifths of the cost required by feeding the high-priced concentrates. Not only so, but a better quality of pork is obtained, the hogs are kept in the best possible sanitary condition, are less liable to disease, and they get the exercise so necessary to their best development, and, above all, the dirty pen is avoided.

Rotation.

The same crops should not be grown on the different lots from year to year, but a rotation should be followed that will preserve an equilibrium in the plant food supply. In this way the soil can be greatly improved.

Impairment of Fecundity.

It has been proven that the fecundity of hogs (and other animals, too) may be greatly impaired by too much corn. It is believed that several breeds of hogs have deteriorated in prolificacy by the over-feeding of corn.

Conclusions as to Possibilities of the South for Hog Raising.

There is no reason why the South should not be the greatest pork-producing section on the continent and sell millions of dollars worth of hogs annually instead of buying the greater part of its bacon in the West. It is only necessary to take advantage of our natural resources and to mix brains and energy with the venture, to transfer the greatest swine-breeding section of the world from the Middle West to the South. We can raise more crops and the grazing period is longer. Then, it is a well-known fact that hogs do not grow nor fatten as rapidly in cold weather as in warm. In other words, it takes more feed to produce a pound of pork in a cold climate than in a warm one, for in the colder sections a large portion of the concentrates fed is consumed in keeping the body at a normal temperature.   LESLIE D. KLINE.

Frederick Co., Va.

THE SALE IN PROGRESS.

THE REDUCTION SALE OF

Live Stock at the Agricultural College and Experiment Station, Blacksburg, Virginia.

Editor Southern Planter:

The last two issues of the Southern Planter have contained advertisements and very complimentary announcements of the Reduction Sale of the surplus pure-bred stock of the Agricultural College, Blacksburg. This sale occurred the day before Thanksgiving, just as our December issue was going to press, therefore, a report of it was not made. We are now pleased to make a general report of this initial effort on the part of the Virginia Agricultural College to disperse her surplus from the herds of pure-bred cattle and Berkshire swine.

In the first place, we desire to call attention to the fact that preparation for this sale was ideal and embodied all the features of the up-to-date popular auction of blooded stock. Complete preparations were made for seating the crowd, with the usual sale ring and other features advantageous to the rapid and systematic selling of stock. Every animal had a number on it corresponding to the number in the catalogue of the pedigrees of the animals sold. That splendid auctioneer, Col. H. L. Igleheart, of Kentucky, was head auctioneer, assisted in the ring by Cols. Roy P. Duvall, of Stephensons, Va.; and Byrd Anderson, of Blacksburg, Va. The sale was very largely attended by the best farmers and breeders of the State, numbering about 400. The advantages of such an attendance—very largely of men who had never visited the Virginia Agricultural College or been in any kind of touch with it before—is evident to all.

After a short address of welcome by the President, Dr. Barringer, remarks by Dr. Walter J. Quick, who succeeded Professor Soule, and also short talks by Cols. Igleheart and Duvall, the sale began with the former in the box.

The selling commenced with the Berkshires at 10 A. M. They numbered forty-five, and were sold within two hours, after which adjournment was had for one hour to partake of the magnificent Thanksgiving spread presented by the V. P. I. to the farmers in attendance, among whom were many of the prominent men of the State. It has seldom been our pleasure to attend a more pleasant and social Convention than the Thanksgiving dinner on the occasion of the V. P. I. Reduction sale at the barns of the Agricultural College Farm. The implements had been moved out of the way and in their stead, on the large implement floor, were spread the tables for the accommodation of the sale guests. It presented a magnificent opportunity for meeting of old friends, renewing and extending acquaintances, and exchanging ideas relative to stock breeding, care and management, and we earnestly believe that this occasion is one that can be repeated to the mutual advantage of the farmers and the Agricultural College. There can be no more ideal way of disposing of the surplus increase of the ten or twelve herds and flocks now owned by the Institution for the very commendable purpose of educational instruction and experimentation, now so large that the increase will make a very creditable one-day sale each year. The time selected for this sale has certainly been ideal, and should come to be known as a time for the annual gathering of farmers and stock breeders at the V. P. I., and an occasion for thanksgiving on the part of all concerned.

But as to the results of the sale, the Berkshires, selling before noon, made an average of almost $20, which is certainly not bad when the fact is taken into consideration that nearly all were pigs of April, May and June farrow. They were certainly a magnificent lot—not a bad animal in the whole farrowing. Only five head were yearlings. Nearly every one seemed well pleased, the more so as the day advanced, and each studied his purchases of the forenoon.

In the afternoon all were filled with hearty good cheer and re-assembled at the sale ring for the dispersion of the Holstein-Friesians, Jerseys and Shorthorns. The sale commenced with No. 4, a young Holstein cow, with a baby at foot that had just appeared on the scene the morning of the sale. Bidding was lively, and even spirited, from the first. This number brought $135, and went to the bid of Dr. Charles G. Cannaday, of Roanoke, Va., who purchased several others and had the honor of topping the Holstein part of the sale, as he had also done on the occasion of the selling of the Berkshires in the forenoon. The Holsteins made an average of about $100, which was all that could have been expected, since over half of the offering were young animals of breeding age. Other strong. buyers were R. P. Johnston, of Asheville, N. C., who secured five head; T. L. Ross, Elamsville, Va., and S. M. Zink, Christiansburg, Va.

The Jersey sale followed the Holstein immediately, the average prices running not quite as high as those of the Holsteins, due likely to the somewhat less valuable offering, and the further fact that two quite young bulls were sold, no Holstein bulls having been offered. Again, as with the Holsteins, Dr. Cannaday, mentioned above, topped the sale, purchasing two of the best. Other good Jersey buyers were E. V| Southall, Jetersville, Va.; J. Coles Terry, Bent Mountain, Va.; J. H. Swisher, Salem, Va., and S. M. Zink, Christiansburg.

The offering of Shorthorns was smaller than either of the other breeds, nearly half the number being young bulls. This left but few animals to interest the breeders of this class of cattle, therefore, representatives to make a good price for the offerings were not present. However, they all sold at the very low average of $80, and every purchaser may consider himself to have bought wisely and well of this class of cattle. The future for the dairy Shorthorns, especially in the old Shorthorn State of Virginia, is destined to be much brighter than the past. This part of the sale was topped by W. J. Burlee, of Whitemarsh, Va., who also purchased the majority of the Shorthorns offered. The other purchasers were C. Henderson, J. T. Hardwick, and J. Coles Terry.

We congratulate the College on this first effort to inaugurate the selling of surplus stock by auction. It cannot fail, if followed up, to bring the College and Station more closely in touch with the farmers and stock breeders of the State—a much needed thing to insure the splendid opportunities afforded by the College being availed of by our farmers' sons. In the past the agricultural students have been few in number compared with the whole body, and have had the least facilities afforded them for becoming enthused in the work. The erection of the new Agricultural Hall and Barns has provided the finest accommodation for a large body of students in agriculture and elevated the dignity of that side of the College to a par with that of the engineering side of the College. The new President, Dr. Barringer, is determined that nothing shall be lacking in the Agricultural Faculty and appliances to make the students in that branch feel that they are the equals of any in the College, and this will, we doubt not, soon lead the young men of the farming classes to seek the advantages offered. These sales will also have a good result in educating farmers themselves to become better judges of live stock, and thus ensure the advancement of good farming in the State. Not until the State becomes essentially a live stock producing State can we hope to see agriculture as prosperous as it ought to be in a section so blessed by natural conditions as ours is.

FINISHING BEEF CATTLE.

(Continued from December issue.)

The cost price of these cattle was $4.10 per 100 pounds,

or just the same as those finished in the stall. The least cost for food was with the silage fed group, the stover lot being second, and the hay lot last. It is quite remarkable that considerable profit was made by these animals on a margin of 25 cents. The straight silage group made a profit of $16.67 compared with a loss of $15.66 for the hay fed group. On a margin of 50 cents, all the groups made a good profit, with the exception of the hay group, which fell behind by $2.20. On a margin of 75 cents, the profit was especially good with the straight silage group with a total of $47.47 to their credit. On a margin of $1.00, the profit for the straight silage group was $63.32; for the hay group, $27.00; for the stover group, $57.30, and for the silage and grain group, $49.40. On a margin of $1.00, the profit from the stockers was $197.02 as compared with a profit of $26.63 for those finished in the stall. In other words, the profit on the stall fed cattle was less than one-seventh as much as was obtained from the stockers on the same margin.

It should be stated in this connection that the cost of labor has not been charged to the stockers, nor have they been credited with the manure produced, which, of course, would not be nearly so valuable as that obtained from the stall fed cattle, owing to the marked difference in the amount of grain fed. If the twenty cattle in this lot had all been fed on silage and had done equally as well as the group confined to this ration, they would have made a profit of $253.28, or $12.66 per head. In this connection it is worthy of note that if all the cattle had been fed on timothy hay, the profit would have been $108, or $5.40 per head. Surely, these facts demonstrate most graphically the wonderful efficiency of silage if judiciously fed as a ration for stockers during the winter, either with or without grain.

Summary of Results for 1905-'06 and 1906-'07.

In conclusion, a summary of the results of feeding 124 head of cattle is presented. Sixty-eight of these cattle were fed to a finish in the stall, and fifty-six were carried through as stockers and finished on grass. The average of the results obtained with such a large number of cattle should be fairly reliable. The figures for both years correspond quite closely and show straight silage, or silage and grain to be the most economical ration for use with stockers in the winter. Moreover, very much larger profits can be secured from handling stockers with the price of foodstuffs as charged in this report than can be anticipated from stall feeding. This does not mean that stall feeding cannot be practiced in some sections with advantage where grass is at a premium or unavailable. It is proper to reiterate that while the cost of finishing in the stall is practically twice as much per pound of gain as on grass that the figures are presented in an unfavorable light to the stall finished cattle. These figures also seem to justify the fact that cattle fed on silage yield a superior quality of beef, do not drift materially when shipped long distances to market, and kill out a good percentage of dressed meat as compared with animals finished in the West on corn. These results also show that on a margin of $1.00, and without taking into consideration the value of the manure or the cost of labor, stall feeding can be practiced in many sections advantageously, even when the animals are charged the highest market prices for the foodstuffs utilized. On the other hand, cattle handled as stockers will produce a considerable quantity of manure and may be made to consume cheap forms of roughness made on the farm, will make large

seed meal group, 1.80 pounds; the corn and cob meal and cotton seed meal group, 1.81 pounds, and the corn meal and cotton seed meal group, 1.73 pounds. These results were affected but little by the hogs following the cattle,

Prize-Winning Red Poll Herd, Virginia State Fair, 1907. Owned by George Ineichen & Sons, Geneva, Ind.

profits on a margin of 50 cents, and will even make fair profits on a margin of 25 cents, when pasture is charged to them at the rate of $1.25 per acre.

These facts are such as to justify us in recommending farmers generally to build silos and utilize silage in their winter feeding operations for practically all classes of cattle, as we believe it can be fed to advantage to calves and yearlings and cattle to be finished either in the stall or on grass. The construction of a silo is not a costly operation and it furnishes food for several months in the cheapeast and easiest form to handle and convey to live stock. It is palatable, easy of digestion and assimilation and is highly relished by all classes of live stock. It is made from a crop that is more widely cultivated than any other in America and solves the difficult problem of securing satisfactory substitutes for grass in sections where the latter does not thrive well. The results, taken all in all, justify the high value we have placed on silage, and it is believed that its extensive ultilization will result in revolutionizing the animal industry of the South.

Conclusions.

1. The results of the trials presented in this report coincide quite closely with those of previous investigations and emphasize more than ever the importance of grass as an adjunct in finishing cattle in the Appalachian region.

2. The results substantiate our previous claims of the high feeding value of silage and justify us in urging farmers in the South to utilize it more extensively as a roughness for cattle which are to be finished in the stall or carried through the winter as stockers and fattened on grass.

3. Owing to the laxative tendency of silage, it has been found advisable to feed a small amount of dry roughness. From two to three pounds of shredded stover or timothy hay have proven ample and, in view of the gains secured, we would not advise the use of larger amounts when the silage is of first class quality.

4. The gains per head per day for the stall fed cattle were quite satisfactory. The ear corn and cotton seed meal group made 1.66 pounds per head per day for the entire period of 149 days; the shelled corn and cotton

which indicates that when a ration of concentrates is properly adjusted there will not be much waste.

5. There was enough difference in the gains obtained in this experiment to justify shelling the corn, but it is a question whether the practice would be profitable one year with another. The gains from corn meal and corn and cob meal were practically the same as those obtained from whole corn, and would not justify the expense incident to grinding the grain.

6. It is again noteworthy that though the cattle consumed approximately three pounds of cotton seed meal per head per day the health of the hogs following them was not affected in any way.

7. In order to secure a fair profit from the stall feeding of beef cattle when no consideration is taken of the manure, it would be necessary to have a margin of at least $1.00 at the prevailing prices charged for the foodstuffs in this trial.

8. It has generally been thought that silage fed cattle would shrink badly when shipped long distances. The actual loss per individual on the cattle shipped to Jersey City was 41.2 pounds, whereas, practical shippers from this section estimate the average shrinkage at from sixty to seventy pounds.

9. As this lot of cattle dressed out 56.9 per cent. of meat of fine quality in which the fat and lean were well blended and equal to that from Western bullocks fed on corn, there is no justification for the opposition to the use of silage for the finishing of beef cattle.

10. Of the cattle fed as stockers, the group receiving straight silage made 1.06 pounds of gain per head per day; the hay group, .27 of a pound; the stover group, .08 of a pound, and the silage and grain group, 1.22 pounds. When placed on pasture the silage fed group made an average gain per head per day of 1.91 pounds; the hay fed group 2.19 pounds; the stover group, 2.85 pounds, and the silage and grain group, 1.58 pounds.

11. The average results of both stall feeding and grazing show that the silage fed group made a gain of 1.43 pounds per head per day; the hay group, 1.11 pounds; the

stover group, 1.30 pounds, and the silage and grain groups, 1.38 pounds.

12. The silage fed group made a pound of gain at a cost of 4.28 cents; the hay fed group, at a cost of 6.45 cents; the stover group at a cost of 4.23 cents, and the silage and grain group at a cost of 4.92 cents. These figures show emphatically the economy of silage as a straight ration for stockers when properly made and preserved.

13. It is apparent from these results that cattle fed as stockers and fattened on grass can be handled on a much narrower margin than those fed in the stall. In this experiment a fair profit was made on a margin of 25 cents, and an excellent profit on a margin of 50 cents. On a margin of $1.00, the profit from the stockers was $197.02 as compared with a profit of $26.63 with those finished in the stall.

14. The figures for both years correspond quite closely and show that straight silage or silage and grain is the most economical ration for use with stockers in the winter. Moreover, that the handling of stockers and finishing them on grass is the most economical practice to pursue in sections where good grazing is available.

15. The cost of making a pound of gain was practically twice as much with the stall fed cattle as with those handled as stockers, but the conclusion should not be drawn from this statement that stall feeding will never be a profitable practice.

16. These facts justify us in recommending farmers to build silos and utilize silage in their winter feeding operations, and it is believed that its extensive use will give a new impetus to animal industries throughout the South.   ANDREW M. SOULE.

SCRUB vs. PURE-BRED CALVES FOR FEEDING.

Editor Southern Planter:

The article by "P." in your November issue relative to the comparative profits in feeding scrub and pure-bred cattle is certainly the most interesting, complete and convincing comparison of the two lines of cattle raising I have ever read. It shows conclusively what I have known all the time—that there is much greater profit in raising pure-bred than scrub cattle where you keep cows and raise your own calves. It, however, fails to get at the particular situation I asked for information upon—i. e., does it pay to keep full-blooded cows a whole year to produce one full-blooded calf when I can buy thrifty scrub calves at $3 each at weaning time? I know from five years experience that there is good money in buying these calves and raising them; but if I can make more by keeping the full-blooded cows to raise the calves instead of paying $3 for the scrubs I would adopt that plan. "P." asks for an estimate of cost and value of these calves after being kept until ready for the butcher. "P.'s" figures as to what his full bloods and high grades weigh and sell for are so far above anything I have ever seen accomplished in this section that I am ashamed to quote my "scrub" figures against his, but as information is what I am after I will give my experience, which is about the same as others in this section. I buy calves in the spring or early summer at from six weeks to four months old at from $2 to $5; they average $3. I put them on bluegrass lawn and feed bran or shorts for a few

weeks—not over $1 worth—to get them started off after being taken from the cow; then turn into pasture of native grass—herds grass, broom straw, weeds, etc.—and give no further attention until late fall, except to salt. As the crops are harvested they have the run of these fields all winter as well as growing rye, oats, etc. About November first they are usually housed in open shed at night and fed rough feed, such as wild grass hay, wheat, oat and rye straw; corn stover (corn cut down, ears taken off and cut up) and sorghum hay, but no grain. No account of the number of pounds fed is kept, but the feed they consume would be well priced at $5; in fact, on account of most of its rough and bulky nature would be hard to sell at all. About May first they are again put on native pasture. In the fall they are sold at about eighteen months old for $18 to $20 each. They have thus cost me about $8, exclusive of the pasture, for which I get $9 to $12, and a good price for a lot of rough feed. The manure made in winter is carefully saved and I figure pays me well for all work attending to and feeding them, and as I can easily carry twenty-five or thirty each season on my 150-acre farm I think it pays me, and my farm is increasing in fertility all the time.   "RETRAC."

DUAL PURPOSE CATTLE—RED POLLS AGAIN.

Editor Southern Planter:

Just to keep my good friend, Mr. Massey, from going wrong—a thing he doesn't often do—I want to say a word or two about the dual purpose cow. Its distinctive feature of milk and beef is illustrated by the Red Poll, Mayflower, that in the six months' test at Buffalo beat all the Jerseys, Holsteins, Brown Swiss and French Canadian in butter and yet took on flesh like a beef animal while doing so. To further illustrate, the cow 4475 Brace was a great milker, yet her heifer calf, 10946 Armlet, won first in her class at Norwich Fat Stock Show, weighing 1672 pounds at two and a half years of age; and another of her calves, 9169 Buckle, took first prize on another occasion, weighing 1629 about the same age. 2213 Gleaner, a great dairy animal, gave 14,189 pounds of milk in twelve months and two of her calves, twins, were entered at different stock shows and both were unbeaten in their respective classes, the steer weighing, at one year and five months old. 1,238 pounds; two and a half years old, 1,732, and the next year, 2,153 pounds. This, I submit, is what the farmer wants—a cow that gives a fine flow of rich milk and drops a calf that makes a good beef animal.

In these days of specialists, we are apt to go too far. The farmer, however, is not ready to give up the country doctor who may be regarded as a dual purpose blessing. Mr. Massey would not advise giving up the country doctor because in some cities good specialists have been developed. Neither should he wish the farmer to lose that other dual purpose friend—the Red Poll—that will bless him with milk, butter and beef all at the same time.

Brother Massey, I know, combines the wisdom of years with that elasticity of mind which shows that he is young yet and still learning. and I hope, if I have understood him aright, he will make amends to the Red Poll and the farmer, whom in other matters he has so much helped.

Albemarle Co., Va.   SAML. B. WOODS.

"A PLEA FOR DEVON CATTLE."

Editor Southern Planter:

That Devon cattle have not been more generally written about and advertised in the agricultural journals of the country has been a surprise to the writer. I do not mean that they do not have a wide distribution, for they can be found in nearly all the States of the Union, but lit-

the less good. They are very deceiving in their weights; they are low to the ground; are smooth, compact, and no flabby parts; well filled up with rich, well-marbled meat, less offal than almost any other breed, often dressing fifty-five to sixty per cent. of live weight. As dairy cattle, they are amongst the best, so far as quality is concerned, while the quantity may not be as large as some

"ON THE BANKS OF THE RIPPLING ALABAMA."
Devon Cows and Heifers on Wilcox Stock Farm. Owned by Pritchett & McDaniel, Camden, Ala.

tle is ever said about them. The Devon is one of the oldest breeds in the United States, and, as one writer says, "No doubt, the first furrow turned on the shores of Massachusetts was turned with a Devon ox at the plow; many of the Pilgrim fathers coming from Devonshire and no doubt, brought the red cow of that country with them." That the Devon should be so seldom written about or advertised in our leading farm journals is surely not because the breed has no merits to bring before the people. When we think what the breed has done in many sections to build up the scrub cattle of the country in which they have been introduced, both in the beef and dairy lines, it is certainly worthy of mention among the noted breeds. The great power of the Devon to effect speedy improvement in beef and dairy qualities is the outcome of singular prepotency, and this prepotency is based largely on two things—first, long purity of breeding; second, its stamina. This prepotency rests as much on the stamina of the breed as on its ancient lineage. Have you ever looked studiously on a herd of Devon cows going or coming from pasture? Then you have noticed the lively, easy carriage and the proud tread of the males and stately bearing of the females, the poise of the head, the clearness of the eye—all these things have spoken to you of vigor which, next to long purity in breeding, is the greatest guarantee of propotency.

One may ask, Are the Devons well adapted to all sections of the country? I answer, yes, for on the bleak hills of Maine as well as the sand dunes of Florida, on the ranches of Texas, they seem to thrive wherever put, showing that they suit all sections. Are they a beef breed? I again answer, yes. While they do not grow as large as some of the other breeds, the quality of the beef is none

of the noted dairy breeds, the quality of the milk has no superior, making the best of butter. Cows making fourteen to sixteen pounds of butter a week are very common among them, and this on grass alone. I claim for the Devon that they will make as much beef per acre on grass or per bushel of feed consumed as any breed will do, and, for milk and butter, I claim the same. They are easy keepers, good rustlers, always in good heart, and respond readily to good feed, and care. So I claim for the Devon the three B's—Beauty, Beef, Butter—and the best of milk for family use, making them the true farmer's cow and general purpose breed.

Newark, Ohio.　　　　　　　　J. F. SISSON.

CATTLE QUARANTINE—NOTICE FOR THE STATE OF VIRGINIA.

Notice to Cattlemen, Transportation Companies and Others Operating in Virginia.

Open Season.—On and after the fifteenth day of December, 1907, until the fifteenth day of March, 1908, cattle originating in the counties below the quarantine line in the State of Virginia, against Texas cattle fever, may be moved for purposes other than immediate slaughter, provided the said cattle have first been inspected at the point of origin, by a duly authorized inspector of the State of Virginia, or an authorized inspector of the Bureau of Animal Industry, Washington, D. C., and the said cattle have been pronounced free from infection (cattle ticks) by the said inspector, and after the said inspector has given his written permission allowing the said cattle to be thus moved.

Exception 1.—If the said cattle ae to be moved from a farm which is under special quarantine, and the said cattle are not for immediate slaughter, then the said cattle may be moved upon inspection, as above described, but must be a_{gain} quarantined on the farm to which they are moved, and must not be moved above the State quaran tine line.

Appointment of Local Inspectors for the Counties.

Notice.—Any county or vicinity can have a good local

least trouble of any. I find they are the easiest to get rid of. It is the little gray or red mite that makes the mischief for me. They do their work mostly at night when the hens are on the roost by crawling on them and sucking their blood. And when hundreds of them get on one hen they are pretty sure to have a telling effect in a short time. They take the very life out of a fowl. They

Brown Swiss Cattle. Prize-Winners at the Virginia State Fair, 1907. Owned by McLaury Bros., Portlandville, N. Y.

cattle man appointed as inspector for the said territory, if the name of the said man to be appointed is sent to the State Veterinarian's office at Burkeville, Virginia, with a written recommendation from the Supervisors of the said county, or from the Chairman of the said Board of Super- visors, requesting that the said man be appointed as local cattle inspector, to be paid for his work either by the cat- tle owners or the county. Upon receiving such a request and recommendation from the Supervisors, the State Veterinarian will commission and instruct the said local man as local cattle inspector at once. By order of the Board of Control.   J. G. FERNEYHOUGH,

                 State Veterinarian.

THE TROUBLESOME INSECTS.

Editor Southern Planter:

Point out to me the man who is positive that there are no insects about his poultry-house, and I will show you a man that in nine cases out of ten is mistaken. Work as you may to rid the house and fowls of these pests and there are most sure to be a few left. In the winter they do not multiply as fast as in the warmer weather, but there is no time when they will not increase if given a chance. A great many poultrymen expend quite large amounts every year for insecticides, and besides this use every other effort to check the increase and to extermi- nate these insects. When the cold weather comes and there are less of them seen about the premises, by a good many, the watchful care is discontinued or partially so. Because they do not seem so plentiful does not mean that they are not there.

A good many speak of lice as being the most trouble- some with their poultry. Lice on my fowls give me the

are very small and work mostly about the vent and under the wings. As a rule they leave the fowls in the morning and hide during the day between boards, in joints, cracks, etc., waiting for night to come out again.

Many, in cleaning the hen-house, give less attention to the roost and nests than any other part. The nesting material will perhaps be taken out and replaced with fresh, and the droppings be removed, but the nest boxes, and under and all around them, and the perches, should be looked to. Generally the reason why this is not done is because to save labor the perches are nailed to the wall or fixed on a frame and the nests are also nailed tight. I often see nests fastened up strongly enough to support a man. This is all wrong. All these fittings should be made and so put up that they can be easily taken down and pulled to pieces and carried outside for a thorough cleaning, for on these there will be found the majority of the insects. When you have the fittings outside of the building sear them over by holding in a blaze a minute or so.

A good insecticide is made of one gallon of kerosene oil and one-half pound of pure naphthaline flakes mixed together. Apply with sprinkling pot or sprayer. There are a number of good powder preparations which if thor- oughly rubbed into the feathers of the fowl will drive off and kill all the body insects. A good dust bath is also very effective for this purpose.

Courtland Co., N. Y.   VINCENT M. COUCH.

Campbell Co., Va., Dec. 16, 1907.

I have been a close reader of the Southern Planter for quite a while and pronounce it the very best paper the farmer of the South can obtain.   T. C. DRNIKARD.

The Poultry Yard.

POULTRY NOTES.

Editor Southern Planter:

I have had many letters during the past few years asking me about the possibilities of poultry raising in the South as a busines. Let us begin the new year with a review of the advantages of the middle South. I came to the State of Virginia in February, 1904 from northeast Indiana where I had been engaged in raising standard bred poultry for many years. I have travelled extensively over the middle, west and northwestern States. I was a State speaker in the Farmer's Institute work for many years and in this capacity came in close touch with many of the leading farmers, breeders and poultrymen of the eight Central States over which I travelled. I studied the various breeds, the conditions of soil, the climate, feed supplies, housing, markets, transportation facilities and charges, pure breds and mongrels and the people, who, after all, make a country what it is, and the various breeds of live stock. The four States, Indiana, Michigan, Illinois and Iowa have more standard-bred poultry than any other four States in the Union. Nearly every State has some fine poultry. New York has some very large and successful plants but in the group of States named thousands of farmers have very fine, large flocks of standard-bred poultry. One firm in northern Indiana paid out last year (1906) $2,350,000 for poultry and eggs.

Naturally we are led to ask, what are the conditions necessary to success with poultry? I will try to answer this question. First, the man or woman. To succeed with poultry means more than the investing of a small sum of money in the business. There is no branch of live small stock husbandry that one can engage in where a small sum of money will yield as large and sure returns every day in the year as poultry. One must be a good judge of poultry, of natural requirements, of natural conditions. The man must be industrious, neat, alert, economical and patient. He must get his information by experience. He must have confidence in himself and his business. He must be willing to do many hard, disagreeable and unselfish things. He must be diligent in business. The slothful man has no place in the poultry world. He must love the business. The hen will pick where she scratches. The man must provide the place for her to scratch and something to scratch for. He must be a generous man, humane, kind and clever. The hen is an early bird. He must be ready to meet her.

The location and farm. This is not so important. Convenience to good transportaion and a dry soil are essential. When I came to my present location, neighbors told me that my fowls would die because there was no gravel or lime about the house or yards. Not over seventy-five rods from the house is a fine gravel bank and oyster shells by the wagon load in the city ten miles away for the hauling. A man with a team will bed all my houses two inches deep with clean, sharp gravel in one day. One ton of oyster shells will furnish all the lime necessary for 1,000 hens for twelve months. A good farmer seldom has a poor farm. If it is poor when he gets it, he will soon make it yield bountifully. A poor farmer seldom has a good farm. If it is good when he gets it, he will soon deplete it of its fertility. Southern farmers should stick a pin here. A good poultryman will make conditions right. The breed. A good strain of any of the standard-bred fowls, well cared for, will return a good income on the investment and labor. For eggs I would select one of the smaller breeds; for broilers and roasters, a heavier breed of a good laying strain, but always and all the time only one breed and that a pure one. Get the best your purse can afford, then select, cull and breed better. Do not keep mongrels or culls. There is no profit in them. Do not pay fancy prices for eggs from "300-egg strains." They will disappoint you about 125 points. The average of the Virginia hens is five dozen per year. Shame on you, in the land of sunshine and honeysuckles. If every hen in Virginia was a good hen and had good feed and care the net income would be three times what it is. My flock of hens (237) laid an average of 154 1-2 eggs during the twelve months and made a net profit of $1.62 1-2 each. This flock will do much better this year because they will not be moved, they will have better care, better housing and the flock is improving every year. I can easily bring them to fifteen dozen per hen. I have no 300-egg hens, and I frankly say that I do not believe that the other fellow has, but everybody can have a better hen than the sixty-egg Virginia hen.

Housing. In the matter of housing we have every advantage over the North and West. We have abundance of good timber, cheap lumber and all material necessary to construct houses and yards for our flocks. Our winters are short and mild. There are more zero days in Indiana, my former home, than there are freezing days in Virginia. The ground is covered with snow and ice more days in northern Indiana than hours in Virginia. Our flocks can have grass and clover nearly every day during the winter months. I have fed poultry seventy days in succession on snow and ice in Indiana. This advantage alone is sufficient to make the difference between profit and loss.

Feeds. It is true that corn, wheat, oats, all grain costs more here than in the West and Northwest, but it takes less and we can grow it here as cheap as it can be grown anywhere if we will make the coditions right.

Who and what is responsible for the conditions as we have them in Virginia? The man. We can grow wheat, rye, crimson clover, red clover, alfalfa, cabbage, turnips, rutabagas, onions, soja beans, cow peas, sorghum, kaffir corn, sunflowers, field peas, potatoes, sweet potatoes, peanuts, beans of all kinds, vetch and rape. Bran, meatmeal, oyster shell and grit cost but little more here, if any, than Northern and Western poultrymen must pay for the same feeds.

Markets. We have better home markets for poultry products than the North and West afford. In addition, we have the same markets that they have. New York, Boston, Hartford, Philadelphia, Baltimore, Washington City are all within easy reach of us at lower freight and express charges than from the great Northwest. Richmond and other Southern cities are not good markets for fancy eggs and fine poultry but there is nothing to prevent poultrymen from shipping to Northern markets. I am shipping eggs North and realize ten to twelve cents per dozen net above Richmond prices. Cold storage eggs are sold in Richmond now as "fresh country" eggs. They are "fresh" from cold storage but were laid last April and May. As long as the consumer will submit to this imposition and be satisfied the producer of fancy fresh eggs must go elsewhere with his goods.

I have written the truth as I see it and know it. What we need in, the South is men who know and understand, and who will do what they know, and understand. We have here every natural advantage. Climate, soil, water, grains, grasses, markets and transportation facilities by land and water, abundance of timber, plenty of sunshine, very little snow and ice, everything nearly ideal, and yet, the Virginia hen lays but one egg in six days.

Where do I put the blame. On the man. With the right kind of men the old mongrel hen would vanish like a snowball in the dominion of His Satanic Majesty and be replaced by standard-bred stock and the South would soon lead the entire country in poultry products and prices.

CAL HUSSELMAN.

PROFITS IN LEGHORNS AND PLYMOUTH ROCKS.

Editor Southern Planter:

In common with others of your readers, I have been interested in following Mr. Husselman's figures for his brown leghorn flock through the past year. His statements have generally been quite clear, but one point I do not understand. Does the cost per hen which he gives at $1.18 1-6 include the feed consumed by the broilers and cockerels which he has sold, or have these been yarded? It strikes me that in a flock of mixed ages on free range where chicks are being raised to replace the old hens and for sale as breeding stock, it is quite impossible to tell what the average consumption of food by the laying fowls really is.

I note that while Mr. Husselman figures a net profit of $1.62 1-2 per hen for eggs at market price, he states that the actual profit from all sales including breeding stock was more than twice this amount, which would mean somewhere near $3.25 per hen. It is only fair to emphasize the fact that every breeder of thoroughbreds can count on some few sales of choice birds at more than market rates, and these should be included in the annual showing so as to encourage the habit of breeding good stock on our Southern farms.

I have been breeding a pure flock of Barred Plymouth Rocks of a very large strain for thirty years, and believe that we now have the oldest flock bred continuously in one ownership that can be found. In different years our flock has varied from a dozen to a hundred. We have often kept accounts of the sales, but never an accurate record of the feed as they are necessarily often fed from the same bin as are the cattle and horses. In the spring of 1896 I brought a dozen hens and one cock from my father's farm to my present home and within a year the gross sales of fowls and eggs amounted to $79 and we had twenty-four instead of twelve females.

This year our record is surprisingly close to that of our leghorn friend, Mr. Husselman. Last winter we were tempted to part with all but about a half dozen of our pullets and began our setting and selling season about April 1, with about twenty-five females, some of them four years old. From April 15th to December 15th the gross cash sales have been $78.44, and we now have on hand seventeen hens, thirty-eight pullets and twenty-two big-framed heavy cockerels. Granting the young stock a value on the farm of $1 each, which is below actual cash worth, we have $60 worth which would far more than cover all that we have expended for feed, though the entire flock had unlimited wheat all summer, purchased at the local mill. The cash sales are thus far a little over $3 for each hen with which we started. It should be stated that we used no incubator and these hens raised all our chicks except for the help of four mongrel sitters which were bought when broody and raised a brood each. Further, a family averaging ten persons has had a moderate supply of eggs and an occasional fowl—one makes a meal—which have not been credited in this account. It will thus be seen that the flock has not been credited with its entire production.

It is only fair to explain that the record is not the result of sales at extreme or fancy prices. We breed a utility flock under farm conditions and have no market among the exhibiting fraternity, although I can seldom buy from them a bird of as much merit as the best I raise. The highest price this season for a single bird has been $3.00, and for a sitting of eggs $1.50. I have paid $5.00 plus $2.25 expressage for a cockerel from the Maine Experiment Station strain to mate with the twenty largest females in our flock, intending to give them a house and half the farm to themselves, and I find this cockerel with eight generations of 200-egg females in his pedigree, to be very much smaller and inferior in general appearance to those which will be disposed of to make room for him.

It would seem that these showings of the actual figures for a large flock of leghorns, a laying breed, and for a small flock of Barred Plymouth Rocks, a general purpose breed, should encourage the more general keeping of standard-bred poultry among our people. It is our purpose to begin next spring with less than fifty females and to steadily develop the poultry feature of the farm either up to the limit of profitable numbers, or as far as it can be attended to by the available help in the family.

As our household has outgrown its present quarters a move to larger buildings at the further end of the same farm will be made in the spring. This may upset our poultry arrangement at the wrong season, but we plan to build separate houses in different parts of the farm so that each flock can have free range and running water.

Vienna, Fairfax Co., Va.   W. A. SHERMAN.

The Horse.

First Prize Young Herd of Morgan Horses at St. Louis Exposition. Owned by the Highlands Farm, L. L. Dorsey, Anchorage, Ky.

The Morgan horse is the oldest and most distinctive reproducing native type in America. They are justly famous for symmetry, docility, intelligence, steadiness and speed.

NOTES.

A fitting tribute to Virginia's largest breeder of light harness horses was the recent election of Samuel Walton, of Falls Mills, as a member of the Board of Directors of the American Trotting Association, at the meeting of the latter organization held in New York City. Certainly Mr. Walton's selection for the position mentioned meets with general approval, as he is not only Virginia's representative breeder of trotters, but the largest also, maintaining at Walton Farm a stud of over one hundred head of richly bred stallions, brood mares and young things, in addition to a large stable of horses in training. Mr. Walton is a man of large affairs and has amassed a competency in business, being now the head of the big railroad contracting firm of S. Walton Company, while he is also a close student of blood lines, and on pedigrees there are few better informed men to be found in this country. Walton Farm with its broad acres and many well-bred horses, has for nearly twenty years past sent out and campaigned a stable of trotters each season and with a goodly share of success, too, as attested by the winning performances of Catherine Leyburn, 2:14 1-4; Skillful, 2:17 1-4; Wilbooka, 2:19 1-4, all of former years; and Margie Z., 2:16 1-4; Maggie Carrell, 2:17 1-4, and others bred at the farm during the past decade. Mr. Walton is president of the Virginia circuit of fairs and race meetings and in that organization his influence is strongly felt.

* * * * * *

Princena, the bay mare, by Sidney Prince, 2:21 1-4, dam Benzeota, by Bendee, son of General Benton, made the most successful campaign during the season just closed that has ever been credited to any Virginia bred trotter, as she began the season perfectly green and starting sixteen times in fifteen weeks she won eleven races, was second four times and once third, retiring with a record of 2:19 1-4. Her campaign being through the Southern Circuit, she was shipped over 1,500 miles and never missed a feed during the whole time. She was raced on nine half mile and five mile tracks, starting in sixty-seven heats, of which she won fifty-two and was close up at the finish of most of the remainder. The remarkable part of the mare's history is that she was driven by no less than five different drivers, all of whom won with her. Princena was foaled in 1902 and bred by Floyd Brothers, Bridgetown, Va., who own her sire and dam. She is a rich bay in color and of a very racy type, and is considered the making of a 2:10 trotter. Her sire, Sidney Prince, 2:21 1-4, the son of Sidney, 2:19 3-4 and Crown Point Maid, who heads the Floyd Farm at Bridgetown, is getting a lot of speed, having some twenty-five or more of his sons and daughters in the list, of which nine made their record in 1907; among them being Princine, 2:10 1-4, Zack, 2:15 1-2, a winner of many races, and O. J. 2:27 3-4, the latter being a two-year-old and the fastest trotter of his age yet bred in Virginia.

* * * * * *

The family of Bingen, 2:06 1-4, in the ripeness of its fame, is very popular at Fredericksburg, Va., among its firmest advocates being Col. W. L. Laughlin, of the Exchange Hotel; A. Randolph Howard, the banker and horse show patron; Count Raoul d'Adhemar, the courtly Parisian, who presides over beautiful Moss Neck Manor on the banks of the Rappahannock; A. B. Lewis, of Wyldewood

Farms, who has offices in Wall Street, New York, and D. Scott Quinten, now director of affairs of a big Fredericksburg manufacturing concern, but formerly well known as developer of the crack trotter, Favonia, 2:15 1-4, and other Grand Circuit winners.

During the season of 1906 and 1907 Col. Laughlin bred his best mares to Admiral Dewey, 2:04 3-4, while quite recently he has puchased from Dr. J. C. McCoy, of Kirkwood, Delaware, owner of that great young sire, the black colt, foaled May 7, 1907, by Admiral Dewey, dam Avina, 2, 2:19 1-2, by Palo Alto, 2:08 3-4, son of Electioneer. The youngster is a well-formed, handsome colt, and being so richly bred it is likely that the son of Admiral Dewey will be kept entire. Col. Laughlin has claimed the name "Alto Dewey" for this colt and hopes to see him develop speed and race horse quality like his sire, Admiral Dewey, the son of Bingen, 2:06 1-4, and famous old Nancy Hanks, 2:04, by Happy Medium.

Count d'Adhemar owns Baron Bingen, the bay horse, by Bingen, dam Ilinda, by Baron Rogers, 2:09 3-4 a trotter, also a blue ribbon winner in the show ring. This well-bred son of Bingen will be further developed for speed, then probably be marked and ultimately retired to the stud at Moss Neck Manor, where some well-bred brood mares are owned, among the latter being Little Queen, 2:25 3-4, a daughter of Lord Jenkinson and others.

At the Wyldewood Farms of Mr. Lewis you can see both well-bred trotters and one of the greatest collection of Jersey cattle in America, headed by the famous bull, Stockwell, for whom Mr. Lewis paid $11,500 at auction during the early part of the present year, while in the herd of over 250 head are several cows that represent an investment of over $500 each. J. T. Carpenter, who was long with the Hood Farm, at Lowell, Mass., has charge of all these cattle and the New Englander is kept very busy looking after them, too. M. F. Hanson, who developed Clarion, 2:15 1-4, and other Virginia bred horses is the farm trainer now. Hanson is wintering Bow Axworthy, 2:21 1-4, one of the handsomest sons of his great sire, Axworthy, 2:15 1-4; an unnamed black mare, 4, by Sable Wilkes: Supremacy, 2:29 1-4, while the remainder of his stable is made up of the New England bred horses Kitty Kremlin, the big chestnut mare, by Kremlin, 2:07 3-4, out of Edgewater Belle, dam of Edgemark, 2:16, by Edgewater; Tilka, bay mare, by Arion, 2:07 3-4, dam La Jolla, dam of Binjolla, 2:17 1-4, by Advertiser, 2:15 1-4; Lisa N., bay filly, 3, by Bingen, dam La Jolla, and a couple of yearlings, both by Bow Axworthy, one being out of Kitty Kremlin, and the other from Louella, the dead daughter of Electioneer. Lisa N. is the pride of Hanson's stable and he thinks she will make a very fast mare. A filly of exquisite quality and finish, the daughter of Bingen, was a blue ribbon winner at the Wissahickon Horse Show of 1906. La Jolla, the dam of Tilka and Lisa N., is thought a lot of at the farm and her foal of 1907, a bay colt

"Buster Brown" 30777, the Great 6-Year-Old Percheron Stallion, Owned by Mr. John F. Lewis, LynnWood, Va.

by Admiral Dewey, is far more highly valued than any other youngster on the place, as he is handsome, well-formed and shows the disposition to trot naturally. La Jolla cost the late J. Malcolm Forbes $2,500 as a yearling and but for an attack of distemper, which caused her retirement, would have been a very fast mare, but she seems destined, however, to make a very great producer, as was her dam, Sally Benton, 2:17 3-4, and her grand dam the great Sontag Mohawk. La Jolla was bred in 1907 to Bow Axworthy and the comely gray mare appears to be with foal to that son of Axworthy and Mystic, the dam of Fred Kohl. 2:07 3-4, by Nutwood.

* * * * *

Thriving and popular, and now, as for years past, one of the most important members of the Virginia Horse Show Circuit, the Orange Horsemen's Association, with headquarters at Orange, Va., is an the top wave of prosperity, has with a nice balance of ready cash in the treasury, the grounds and buildings are paid for and kept in good condition. The officers of the Association for 1908 are: John T. Lightfoot, president; H. O. Lyne, George S Shackleford and W. P. Jones, vice-presidents; L. S. Ricketts, secretary and treasurer. The Board of Directors is made up of W. W. Sanford, Thomas Atkinson, William Du Pont, W. C. Williams, Sr., J. F. Van Derhoff, George Zinn, H. T. Holladay, Jr. and R. D Browning.

Nottoway Co., Va., Dec. 17, 1907.
I consider the Southern Planter a necessity.
M. C. FOWLER.

Wolfe Co., Ky., Dec. 16, 1907.
The Southern Planter is the best farm paper I have ever taken, and I would not be without it.
L. D. MITCHELL.

Miscellaneous.

THE FARMERS' WINTER COURSE AT THE VIRGINIA POYTECHNIC INSTITUE.

Editor Southern Planter:

Two distinct problems in agricultural teaching now confront the Land Grant Colleges. The first is the technical preparation of men to advance the sciences on which the art of agriculture rests, and the other is to devise the best means of bringing before those who practice the art of agriculture—the farmers—the facts obtained by scientific investigation. Three methods have been used in reaching the farmer: First, agricultural literature, including agricultural journals of all types and Experiment Station bulletins, second, the Farmer's Institutes, and third, the Farmer's winter course. The first methods have the great advantage of wide distribution, and nothing can take their place. The Farmer's Institute is expensive if carried on a large scale, but it has the advantage of personal contact.

Both of the preceding, in spite of their many advantages, are deficient in one element—they cannot carry with them, even with best illustrations and drawings, a proper idea of the apparatus and scientific plant from which the truths they enunciate have been drawn. The Farmers' winter course, as given in the Land Grant Colleges, is the final and last step of a graded system. Here those attending see the expensive barn and herds, the proper milking, weighing, and testing of milk. Spraying and pruning are shown in the large college orchard, crop pests in museum cases. forcing methods in the greenhouses, etc. It is of advantage chiefly to those who have thought and studied. Coming as it does annually during the farmers' period of rest in mid-winter, several week's time can be given, and experience has proven these courses to be of the highest advantage.

At the Virginia Polytechnic Institute such a course was inaugurated this winter for the first time. Eighteen counties in the State were represented by one or more farmers, as follows: Albemarle, Alexandria, Bedford, Botetourt, Campbell, Culpeper, Floyd. James City, Montgomery, Nelson, Nottoway, Orange, Pittsylvania, Powhatan, Prince Edward. Shenandoah. Smythe and Wythe. It was a body of men of unusual intelligence, and many of them of considerable wealth. About half of them secured accommodation at the hotels and in private families, but the crowd who seemed to enjoy it most were those who went together into the Agricultural Building. Some of the large lecture rooms of this building were emptied, and iron beds placed in them in English dormitory fashion. In the same building were reading rooms with all the agricultural journals of the country, bulletin rooms, etc. Several times a week projectoscope lectures, and other methods of entertainment were given at night. In the basement floor of the same building, a large room was used for stock judging, where at one time as many as six Jerseys and six Guernseys were exhibited side by side for farmer students to work on with score cards. In the rear of this building is a battery of five greenhouses, and here the farmers in small sections, were taught the proper and improper

methods of preparing spraying mixtures—Bordeaux, lime sulphur, etc. At the barn a twelve horse power engine was used in demonstrating the practical use of corn husking and shredding machinery, ensilage cutters, etc. All this Demonstration work was done in the afternoon, while in the morning of the same days lectures were given on the principles underlying each procedure.

The farmers boarded at the college mess at the rate of $3.00 per, week, and they seemed to enjoy very much the accommodations provided. The course of lectures was so arranged that the general principles of agriculture came first, then horticulture was added, then animal husbandry, dairying, etc. A general idea of the course is shown in the following:

Prof. Davidson: Stable Manure—Commercial Fertilizers—Nitrogen and Potash—Home-mixed Fertilizers.

Prof. Holden: Origin of Soils, etc.

Dr. Ellett: Soil Physics—Soil Chemistry, etc.

Prof. Carrier: Silo Construction—Filling Silos—Soiling—Forage Crops—Crop Rotation—Cropping Systems.

Prof. Price: Locating Orchard—Pruning Vineyard—Growing Orchard—Spraying—Pruning—Orchard Pests—Fruit Harvesting.

Dr. Quick: Breeding of Cattle—Breeding Principles—Feeding Principles—Stock Judging.

Dr. Spencer: Holsteins, Jerseys, Guernseys, Beef Cattle, Swine and Sheep.

Dr. Ferguson: Milk Fermentation—Milk Sterilization

Col. Marr: Farm Surveys—Farm Levels—Land Drainage—Hydraulic Rams—Roads and Road Making.

Dr. Spencer: Castration—Examining Horses—Wounds, etc.

Col. Wood: Seed Testing—Plant Propagation—Greenhouses.

Mr. Holdaway: Babcock Test—Pasteurizing—Cheese Making.

Prof. Hutchison: Plat Experiments—Corn Improvement.

Mr. Feyton: Inspection of Barns—Implements—Machinery—Silo Machinery—Silo Filling.

Prof Sanders: City Milk Trade—Butter Making.

Prof Phillips: Orchard Pests—Grain Insects—Healthy Trees.

Dr. Smyth: The Relation of Bird Life to Agriculture: I. Hawks and Owls. II. Insects and Grain-Eating Birds.

The authorities of the Virginia Polytechnic Institute have learned much from the present course. They will be able to make the next one much better. This course during the winter of 1908-9 will begin about the first week in January and last one month. It will be so arranged that the major part of the first two weeks will be general agriculture and agronomy, at the beginning of the third week horticulture, which will last about two weeks, while the last week or ten days will be devoted largely to dairying and dairy practice. In this way a farmer can take all, or if he is a horticulturist or dairyman and wishes to concentrate on these only he can get away in eight or ten days. Judging from the interest elicited from this course, it is belived that the number next year will show a hundred or more men, and in a few years a thousand is a number not impossible, as shown by the results in Pennsylvania and other States.

P. B. BARRINGER, President
Virginia Polytechnic Institute, Blacksburg, Va.

IMPROVEMENT OF TIDEWATER, VIRGINIA, LANDS.
Gloucester County.

Editor Southern Planter:

Some years ago, a systematic study was made of the soils of Tidewater (Gloucester county), Virginia. These investigations covered field and laboratory experiments. Physical analysis showed that these soils were mainly fine sandy loams, consisting of fine sands, silts and clays in varying proportions. Chemical analyses revealed a striking deficiency in phosphoric acid, the highest content in any soil being .006 per cent. There were larger quantities of nitrogen and potash, but these were by no means excessive. Details of these investigations were given the public through your Journal when they were made.

Simultaneously with these investigations in the laboratory field experiments were also made, looking to a solution of the manurial requirements of these soils.

Extensive experiments with nitrogen, phosphoric acid and potash, using them singly, in pairs and altogether, were tried under corn and tobacco. Dried blood, acid phosphate and the various forms of potash furnished the above ingredients. These experiments extended over several years until we were thoroughly convinced of the needs of the different fields on the farm. They showed conclusively that potash in any form was not required for the growth even of these potash-loving plants. Phosphoric acid was the ingredient most emphatically called for. Given these, and there was still a demand for nitrogen for maximum growth. Without phosphoric acid the other ingredients produced no results. These experiments suggested at once a plan of action for future operations. The phosphoric acid must be purchased and the small amount in the soil suggested applications to each crop. The nitrogen could be easily furnished to the soils by the growing of leguminous crops. So a plan was ultimately formulated, which gave us two leguminous crops during a short rotation. Starting with corn as the first crop, the ground is occupied the next year with cow peas or soja beans as the summer crop, followed in winter by wheat, which, in turn, is succeeded by crimson clover, and then back to corn. It reads, condensed, as follows: First crop, corn; second, cow peas or soja beans; third, wheat; fourth, crimson clover. Acid phosphate is used with each of these crops, 100 to 200 pounds to the acre, usually the latter quantity.

A goodly number of Hereford cattle, Southdown sheep, and Berkshire hogs, besides the usual farm complement of horses, colts and mules, are kept, requiring a large quantity of forage to sustain them. The corn is therefore harvested with a corn binder and, when cured, carefully shredded and stored for winter feed. Just here it may be remarked that this has become our main reliance for the maintenance of the mature, dry cattle during the winter and, when properly supplemented with leguminous hays and cotton seed meal, is an excellent ration for fat-

tening steers. We also convert into hay the cow peas, soja beans and crimson clover and feed them all on the farm.

The crimson clover remaining after serving as an early spring pasture for all the stock, is harvested in early May—an unfavorable season, however, for curing hay—and the land immediately broken with heavy, two-horse plows, six to ten inches deep. After thorough pulverization and the application, broadcast, of 200 pounds of acid phosphate to the acre, the corn is planted. It is cultivated with the shoe and disc two-horse cultivators, usually the former, when the plant is young, and the latter, when the corn is large, using the precaution always to see that the discs are not set too deep or too close to the corn, to avoid cutting the roots. The corn crop, as stated above, is harvested with a binder and shredder for feeds.

Just here occurs a fault in our rotation—leaving the corn stubble through the winter without a cover. Some have overcome this by sowing the corn with crimson clover at the last working. Several trials of this practice have proven unsuccessful, and we are yet without a profitable suggestion. While awaiting the next spring, the harvesting of the crimson clover, this corn stubble is thoroughly broken with heavy plows, pulverized and planted in cow peas or soja beans, using a wheat drill, which also distributes the acid phosphate. A bushel of each seed is used per acre. No after cultivation is given these crops. In August or September these crops are converted into hay, save a limited area of each, which is reserved for seed. Soon after peas or beans are cut, the land is cross-broken with a disc harrow and sowed in October in wheat, using a drill to sow the wheat (about one and a quarter to one and a half bushels per acre) and to distribute the acid phosphate. The wheat is harvested with a binder and, when dry, threshed, stacking the straw carefully for winter use. In August such weeds and grasses as may have occupied the wheat field since harvest are removed with a mower and converted into hay. The clean land is at once cross-broken with a disc harrow and, when pulverized, sown in crimson clover (fifteen pounds per acre), using the wheat drill with clover seed attachment, putting out at same time the acid phosphate. An iron roller follows the drill and is followed by a smoothing harrow, which completes the work. Corn, as explained above, succeeds this crop in the spring.

Of course, in addition to this rotation, stable manure is used whenever and wherever we can, using a distributor to spread it over the fields. This manure is distributed from the stables every few days during the growing season, putting it upon any available land; now on the clover field, now on the wheat stubble, and sometimes on the growing wheat. In early spring, when the accumulations of the winter are upon us, we aim to put it on the fields destined for corn—the proper place for stable manure, in true farm economy. Last year 750 loads of thirty bushels each were distributed over seventy-five acres of land.

The Results.

The results of eight years of this practice have been very satisfactory. In the beginning the fields were very thin, having been in cultivation for over 250 years. They rarely produced over ten to fifteen bushels per acre of corn; now great improvement is everywhere apparent and yields of thirty bushels of corn per acre are common to all the fields, the best going much higher. Forty acres of this land has increased its fertility to such an extent as to be successfully planted in alfalfa. Twenty-five acres are still devoted to this crop, while a small field occupied for four years, and from which twenty crops of hay have been harvested, was last year planted in corn in June and no fertilizer used. Positive information of exact yield is not yet to hand, but several of our farmers predicted seventy-five bushels per acre just before harvest. The comparative merits of the two crops—cow peas and soja beans—are often discussed. It has been clearly shown that when harvested for hay before developing seed the results in soil fertility are essentially alike, but if both are permitted to mature seed it will be found that the soja bean has carried from the soil a greater quantity of fertility, because the quantity of seed is greater and the grain itself is much richer in nitrogen than the grain of the cow pea.

Experience in 1905 abundantly corroborates the above. In spring of 1904, two adjoining fields—one of twenty-five acres, the other of thirty-two acres—were planted simultaneously—the former in cow peas, the latter in soja beans—both at the rate of one bushel per acre, put out with a wheat drill. The fields were fairly similar in fertility and received the same preparation. In August, the peas were made into hay. The beans were permitted to mature their seed and were not harvested until late. Both fields made large crops—the yield of beans in seed being enormous. These fields were sown in wheat, after thorough preparation with disc harrow. At harvest the field in cow peas yielded about twenty bushels of wheat per acre, while the field in beans gave a return of about ten bushels. At the time of the harvest of the beans a calculation of the quantity of nitrogen removed by this large crop of seed justified the prediction that there was not enough of this element left in the soil to produce a maximum crop of wheat. The final results fulfilled this prediction.

Care in the selection and planting of the seed of every crop grown, the use of all available home-made manure, aided by every labor-saving implement, coupled with pursuit of the above rotation, will, it is believed, make every acre of land not only very productive, but sufficiently remunerative during the regeneration to give a handsome living to the farmer.

Fearing that the supply of potash, now so heavily drawn on by the increased crops, might be getting low, every few years experiments are made with this ingredient to test the present available quantity.

So far, no indication of a deficiency has been manifested, nor do I believe an application of potash manures will be necessary as long as the crops grown upon the land are fed to stock and the resulting manure carefully returned to the fields.   WM. C. STUBBS.

Gloucester Co., Va.

THE NEED OF THE SOUTH—INTENSIVE NOT EXTENSIVE FARMING.

Editor Southern Planter:

In reading the agricultural journals and bulletins issued by the Experiment Stations, it is a very obvious fact that the most prosperous farmers, and the most successful, are the class that devote their energies to a very small area compared to the great plantations that in ante-bellum days were the pride and the boast of the South.

(Mr. Editor, please note what I say is spoken in regard to the South only).

But circumstances have changed completely. The slave of yesterday has become the lord (?) of to-day. The great plantations with their quarters and overseers are only a memory and the intent of the law is that each human being shall reap the reward of his own labor. The Southern planter in his endeavor to reap the same income as that before the '60's, rented his fields to untutored labor with the result of a complete failure to himself and the tenant. What were once fertile and productive fields were replaced by broomsage and deep washes, and later on by the friendly pine. The tenant moved to more promising fields, and the disappointed landlord saw what was once the pride of his intelligence and the boast of his tongue pass from his hands to satisfy his creditors, and he himself "broke up housekeeping" to live with some of his children or grandchildren, or moved to the town from where, after a few years, he was laid to rest on a stranger's land.

The framework, the skeleton, of the old plantation is still with us. The same sun shines upon us, the same seasons assist our efforts, and the same God listens to our prayers.

We read every day accounts of how some energetic, intelligent person has produced five times the amount per acre upon a small farm through intensive farming and improved methods, that could have been produced through the old plan. The salvation of our South is in the small farm with intensive methods applied. The Northern States with their small farms and intensive cultivation and the disadvantage of long and cold seasons, outrival us in the money value of their productions per acre. With educated minds and improved machinery they laugh us to scorn, notwithstanding our soils are more fertile and our winters milder.

We are pleased to continue in the same unprofitable way and scold at intelligent advice, while we sacrifice our labors to the customs of tradition. Of course, some one will wisely ask, "Wherein is our safety?" Turn your faces toward the North, and there in eternal letters read the answer from Maine to Maryland, and from the Great Lakes southwest toward the Pacific Ocean. Learn from that country where it is not considered a disgrace to one's character and a lowering of one's dignity to labor upon the farm. Our South is inoculated with too great an abundance of that false pride which will not permit one to honestly earn his bread following the plow; we must bury forever our unworthy prejudices against a worthy immigrant, it matters not whether he hail from Continental Europe, or from a distant part of our own Union. And right here I wish to say that I sincerely believe that the Northern and Western farmer who has come among us and made our country his country, is the salt to the whole system. They do not agitate nor do they advocate, but their examples of untiring labor are gradually working a revolution over the entire country. We need more of these living examples, and the finished products of the agricultural colleges and Experiment Stations. They place before our very eyes that of which we read. They are always willing to assist us in whatsoever way they can, with their unselfish advice and assistance. They place before our sight the amount of labor that can be saved through the use of modern machinery.

You of the cold North and you of the far West, we want you, we need you, we invite you, and we will endeavor to make you welcome.

We work (?) too great an area to devote to any single crop the necessary attention. We till too many acres. Our forty-acres-to-one-horse idea should be abandoned and be succeeded by the ten-or-twenty-acres-to-one-horse plan. Is not twenty-five acres enough? Is not fifty enough at the most? Would it not be more profitable and more pleasant to us to plant less acres and work them better? And would it not be a good plan to spend two or three dollars for several clean agricultural journals? Spend a penny for a postal and ask your Agricultural Department and Experiment Stations to mail you their bulletins as issued. Let's diversify our crops; cotton is king we know very well, but it is a tyranical king when we permit it to grow only six and eight hundred pounds seed and lint per acre. I believe the South can have more kings than one. Let's try more of the intensive farming, and, above all, let us try and get more of the Western and Northern farmers among us.

A word in regard to my plan for rotation of crops given in November Planter, and Mr. Percival Hicks' comment upon the same given in December Planter.

I presume from Mr. Hicks' article that he misunderstood my suggestions to some extent, but wish to state that it is with the greatest respect for his judgment that I beg to explain the points that, I am sorry to note, I failed to make clear, and which Mr. Hicks kindly objected to in my rotation. I have not the least doubt that my suggestions are objectionable in Tidewater, Virginia, just as stated by Mr. Hicks, but I think, or rather know, from experience, that they are applicable here in the Piedmont section of North Carolina. He thinks the following of the oats and vetch by peas to be planted in June, I suppose, to be rather late. Possibly June may be too late for the Tidewater country, but I have planted peas as late as July 13th after oats and made a fine crop of hay, as well as having many of the peas to mature. His second objection: We succeed very well following peas with crimson clover. His third objection: Oats and vetch do well in this section after corn. But Mr. Hicks kindly supposes that his first and third objections may not be applicable to North Carolina, and is just as reasonable in regard to his second objection, thus I see Mr. Hicks and I advocate about the same plan wherever the seasons will permit. But I wish to call attention to the fact that in my rotation one can save two crops from the same land every year after the first year, i. e. oats and vetch, and peas the second year, and crimson clover and corn or cotton the following year and so on.

Yet the main point I wished to emphasize was that the land planted in corn producing only fifteen or twenty bushels per acre could be cultivated more remuneratively by substituting peas, oats, vetches, and crimson clover, while the land would be improved also.

I am sure if you can get a farmer to read a single issue of the Southern Planter that he will remain upon your subscription list.

Warren Co., N. C.   H. C. COLEMAN.

DEMONSTRATION FARM WORK IN VIRGINIA.

The following is the report of the Director of Demonstration Farms, Mr. T. O. Sandy, made to the meeting of the Cooperative Education Association on the work done in the State under his direction in the year 1907, together with the report of the individual farmers on the results attained.

"My duties commenced January 15th, 1907, and my report covers from that time to the present.

My territory includes Charlotte, Prince Edward, Nottoway, Amelia, Chesterfield, Appomattox and Dinwiddie Counties.

Total number of Demonstrators 20; Cooperators 25; number of meetings held 27; average attendance, about 100; number of miles travelled by rail 5,863; by conveyance 236.

This work began on a small scale and while seven counties were included only a few Demonstrators could be seen after in each as I had no assistants and had to cover the ground mapped out imperfectly, but enough has been accomplished to determine the sentiment of our people and what could be done to improve agricultural conditions.

I will explain here a Demonstrator is one who agrees to prepare, fertilize, seed and cultivate a certain portion of his farm, following in every particular the directions of the Director. His farm is visited as often as necessary to see that the instructions are understood and carried out.

A Cooperator is one who seeks advice from the Director, follows his method but is not given personal attention unless time permits.

The meetings held were in the interest of this work, trying to impress upon our farmers the importance of getting out of the "old ruts," to renew their energy and to realize there was "life in the old land" yet, and what could be accomplished by a few could be by all if only more interest and energy were put forth.

I have no complaint to make, this Demonstration work which has already been done has proven a success; certainly enough to inspire us to extra efforts and to expand, as men of ability as directors and the financial aid can be procured.

It has been considered best to concentrate this work for the next year in one section of the State so as to obtain the best results and show a decided improvement in conditions, which, we trust, will stimulate the remainder of the State as well as gain the confidence of the skeptical.

Farmers are thinking people and they fully realize they have to work too hard to try experiments. We want it strictly understood our methods are not experimental, but have been put into actual practice right here in our State, and are bearing fruit. For instance, more than one of the Demonstrators assures me their fields of corn have not only attracted the attention of their neighbors, but people from a reasonable distance have driven to inspect, and in many instances applied for seed, so you can readily see the good which the success of these men accomplished—it inspired others.

For corn the land is to be ploughed, in the fall, eight inches deep, following with a subsoil plow breaking from seven to eight inches deeper. Harrow in one ton of lime to the acre. In the spring the land should be disced and gotten as fine as possible. Five hundred pounds of pure raw bone to the acre should be applied broadcast. The corn should be planted about the first of May and worked perfectly flat, with cultivators, after each rain, leaving the ground always with a dust mulch. At the last working seed German clover. This will improve the land for the next year's crop, giving the necessary plant food.

For grass culture the preparation is very much the same, only different dates. The German clover which was seeded in the corn should be ploughed under eight inches deep the following June. The land should be disced and harrowed every ten or twelve days during June and July. Apply broadcast five hundred pounds of pure raw bone to the acre. If possible seed the first week in August twenty-five quarts to the acre of the following mixture: Two parts timothy, two parts herds grass and one part sapling clover, adding three pounds alfalfa seed per acre. The alfalfa is simply to inoculate our soil. All of our lands need inoculation. After the seed is sown the land should be harrowed and rolled both ways. By this method I produced six tons of hay to one acre, which was seeded to see what could be done. We must impress upon our ˏpeople the importance of producing their hay. Within a radius of twenty miles of Burkeville $230,000 was spent for hay alone in one year.

In our Demonstration work we strive to increase the earning capacity of the farmers; to improve their surroundings in every way. We urge them to keep better stock—cattle, horses and hogs—which will enable them to secure and maintain better schools, better roads and improve conditions generally.

I will now read the corn reports for the year from each Demonstrator, showing the results:

Report on corn by one of the Demonstrators, O. E. Peterson, Pamplin City, Appomattox County, Va.:

Number of acres in demonstration? Four. Crop grown on land last year, light crop of clover. When broken for this crop? April 1st. Any after tillage? Subsoiled 14 inches. Condition at planting? Very fine and mellow. Variety of seed planted? "Yellow Dent." Amount of seed furnished by the Department? Three pecks. When planted? May 15th. Width of rows? Three and a half feet. Distance between plants in row? Eighteen inches. Kind of fertilizer used? Pure raw bone. Pounds per acre? Seven hundred pounds per acre. How and when applied? Five hundred pounds of raw bone drilled in before planting, 200 pounds of dissolved bone sown broadcast before last tillage. Was field harrowed or cross harrowed after planting? It was not. Number of times ploughed or cultivated? Four. Implements used? Two-horse spring tooth cultivator. Were peas sown in corn? No, German clover. Yield per acre? Sixty-five bushels. Value per bushel (market price in neighborhood)? Sixty cents. Yield of similar land near by per acre? Thirty bushels. Total value of crop, corn and stover? $181. Expense for fertilizer, cultivation, harvesting and housing? $75. Total profit? $106.50. I will not occupy enough of your valuable space to give in detail all of the reports, but will give names and results of each Demonstrator.

R. W. Payne, Drakes Branch, Va.: Number of acres in demonstration? Five. Yield per acre? Thirty-five bushels. Total value of crop, corn and stover? $150. Cost of fertilizer, cultivation and harvesting? $100. Total profit? $50.

T. O. Sandy, Burkeville, Va.: Number of acres in demonstration? Five. Yield per acre? Seventy-five bushels. Total value of crop, corn and stover? $331.25. Cost of fertilizer, cultivation and harvesting? $86.50. Total profit? $244.75.

Virginia Normal and Industrial Institute, Ettricks, Va.: Number of acres in demonstration? Four. Yield per acre? Forty-one and a quarter bushels. Total value of crop, corn and stover? $175.30. Cost of fertilizer, cultivation and harvesting? $58.80. Total profit? $116.50.

R. B. Stone, Blackstone, Va.: Number of acres in demonstration? Two. Yield per acre? Forty-five bushels. Total value of corn and stover? $79. Cost of fertilizer, cultivation and harvesting? $30.75. Total profit $48.25.

F. M. Rand, Keysville, Va.: Number of acres in demonstration? One. Yield per acre? Twenty-one and a quarter bushels. Total value of corn and stover? $24.94. Cost of fertilizer, cultivation and harvesting? $25.29. Total loss? Thirty-five cents.

T. C. Morton, Rice, Va.: Number of acres in demonstration? Two. Yield per acre? Thirty-three bushels. Total value of corn and stover? $64.55. Cost of fertilizer, cultivation and harvesting? $14.51 Total profit? $50.04.

J. J. Gilliam, Farmville, Va.: Number of acres in demonstration? Four. Yield per acre? Thirty-one and a quarter bushels. Total value of corn and stover? $130. Cost of fertilizer, cultivation and harvesting? $71.24. Total profit? $58.76.

E. A. Irving, Pamplin City, Va.: Number of acres in demonstration? Three. Yield per acre? Forty bushels. Total value of corn and stover? $100. Cost of fertilizer, cultivation and harvesting? $75.50. Total profit? $24.50.

M. M. Hayden, Nottoway, Va.: Number of acres in demonstration? Five. Yield per acre? Sixty bushels. Total value of corn and stover? $155. Cost of fertilizer, cultivation and harvesting? $70. Total profit? $85.

L. S. Jackson, Drakes Branch, Va.: Number of acres in demonstration? Four. Yield per acre? Thirty-five bushels. Total value of corn and stover? $137. Cost of fertilizer, cultivation and harvesting? $50.50. Total profit? $86.50.

B. F. Norfleet, Jetersville, Va.: Number of acres in demonstration? Three. Yield per acre? Twenty-two and a half bushels. Total value of corn and stover? $90. Cost of fertilizer, cultivation and harvesting? $57.56. Total profit? $32.44.

The John A. Dix Industrial School, Dinwiddie, Va.: Number of acres in demonstration? Four. Total value of corn and stover? $123. Cost of fertilizer, cultivation and harvesting? $65.10. Total profit? $57.90.

J. W. Southall, Jetersville, Va.: Number of acres in demonstration? Five. Yield per acre? Twenty-five bushels. Total value of corn and stover? $125. Cost of fertilizer, cultivation and harvesting? $104.50. Total profit? $20.50.

J. A. Hardy, Blackstone, Va.: Number of acres in demonstration? One. Yield per acre? Seventy-six bushels. Total value of corn and stover? $62.20. Cost of fertilizer, cultivation and harvesting? $20.75. Total profit? $41.45.

David Hindle, Amelia, Va.: Number of acres in demonstration? Four. Yield per acre? Eighty-four and seven-tenths bushels. Total value of corn and stover? $299.60. Cost of fertilizer, cultivation and harvesting? $98.61. Total profit? $200.99.

J. L. Bradshaw, Burkeville, Va.: Number of acres in demonstration? One. Yield per acre? Forty bushels. Total value of corn and stover? $40. Cost of fertilizer, cultivation and harvesting? $20. Total profit? $20.

The following reports are on grass:

J. J. Gilliam, Farmville, Va.: Number of acres in demonstration? Three and a half. Yield per acre? Two and a half tons. Market value? $175. Cost of seed, fertilizer, cultivation and harvesting? $32.80. Total profit? $142.20.

T. O. Sandy, Burkeville, Va.: Number of acres in demonstration? Twelve. Total yield? Fifty tons. Market value? $1,000. Cost of seed, fertilizer, cultivation and harvesting, $200.10. Total profit? $790.

T..C. Morton, Rice, Va.: Number of acres in demonstration? Three. Total yield? Nine tons. Market value? $180. Cost of seed, fertilizer, cultivation and harvesting? $53.50. Total profit? $126.50.

Nottoway Co., Va.   T. O. SANDY.

THE VIRGINIA POLYTECHNIC INSTITUTE.

(Agricultural and Mechanical College) Blacksburg.

We have lately had the opportunity of discussing with Dr. P. B. Barringer, the President, the needs and requirements of the Agricultural college in the way of help from the Legislature in order to enable it to do the work for the people of the State which it was created to do. In the past the Legislature has been liberal in providing the money needed to erect the buildings of the college, but these buildings are yet inadequate to provide the accommodations called for by the large number of students who desire to avail themselves of the advantage offered and especially is this so on the agricultural side of the College. The new Agricultural Hall will provide the class rooms, laboratories and lecture rooms; but this building is situated so far away from the Mess hall and dormitories that much time is lost by the students in going backwards and forwards and there is urgent need for the erection of a new dormitory, mess hall and cooking department near to the Agricultural Hall for the boarding and lodging of the agricultural students. The erection of this building would be true economy in the education of these students and would make room for students who want to take the mechanical work of the College in the dormitories and Mess hall now existing, which are in close proximity to the class rooms, lecture halls and shops in which these students pursue their studies. With this further addition to the buildings the College would be placed in a position to handle economically and with proper supervision a much larger number of students and this with economy of teaching staff. A pressing need of the College is also a larger annual appropriation for the upkeep of the buildings and the normal running expenses of the College. With the constant addition to the buildings and the passing of years since the erection of some of these the cost of repairs and insurance has become a heavy item, whilst the great increase in the cost of living and the increased teach staff is now so much more costly as to make the $50,000 annually insufficient to meet the expenses. In these days of education and progress it will not do to increase the burden of the charge on parents who desire to send their sons to the College. This is the "poor man's college" and should continue to retain that character.

It should be so supported as that no farmer in the State should feel that he cannot afford to send one or more of his sons to get the benefit of a technical training for his life work. To enable this to be done the State must give more liberally than it has done in the past. Hitherto the annual grant from the State has been $50,000. This should be increased to at least $75,000. Blacksburg is educating more Virginia students each year than the University of Virginia and the Virginia Military Institute together are doing and yet these two institutions, which are preeminently the finishing schools for the sons of the wealthy classes, are more liberally aided by the State than Blacksburg. We take no exception to the annual grants made to these two institutions, but we do claim and we think with justice that Blacksburg should at least be put on a similar footing with these so far as the State support is concerned. Surely $75,000 a year is not an extravagant sum to ask for educating the sons of the less wealthy class in the community in the technical knowledge required to make them proficient in their chosen calling. Technical education and training is necessarily more costly than simple education in the three "R's" but it is of infinitely more value to the State in increasing values and consequently revenues for the State. Its liberal support by the State is "bread cas. upon the waters." It will return tenfold its cost in a few years time. There is also needed further equipment for the Engineering Department and several other additions to the buildings for the economical conduct of the business of the College. An increase also of the appropriation to the Experiment Station is called for. Prior to the last session of the Legislature the State made no appropriation for the Experiment Station or its work. At that time $5,000 was appropriated. This is a very small sum to set apart for such an important adjunct to the work of the farmer, for to a very great extent his success depends on the work done by the Experiment Stations. The Legislature ought to appropriate at least $10,000 for the Station and this with the Federal grant will then enable a considerable extension of the work being done. We put these facts before the farmers that they may consider the same and bring their influence to bear upon their representatives in the Legislature to have these appropriations made. There is money in the Treasury which the farmers have largely provided. Their special institutions have a claim to be favorably considered and we do not doubt but that they will be so considered if the farmers will urge the point upon their representatives. We would suggest that the President of the State Farmers' Institute should call the officers and members of the Executive Committee together here at Richmond during this month to take these matters into consideration and to arrange for pressing them upon the attention of the Legislature and it would be well if the members of other farmers' organizations, such as the State Horticultural Society, would also meet here at the same time and arrange for cooperative action in reference to all matters affecting their several interests. By united action success in securing what is needed can be assured.

THE

Southern Planter

PUBLISHED BY

THE SOUTHERN PLANTER PUBLISHING CO.,
RICHMOND, VA.
ISSUED ON 1ST OF EACH MONTH.

J. F. JACKSON,
Editor.

B. MORGAN SHEPHERD,
Business Manager.

B. W. RHOADS,
Western Representative, 844 Tribune
Building, Chicago, Ill.

MANCHESTER OFFICE:
W. J. Carter, 1102 Hull Street.

ADVERTISING RATES
Will be furnished on application.

The SOUTHERN PLANTER is mailed
to subscribers in the United States,
Mexico and island possessions at 50
cents per annum; all foreign countries,
$1.00; the city of Richmond and Canada,
75 cents.

REMITTANCES should be made
direct to this office, either by Registered Letter or Money Order, which
will be at our risk. When made otherwise we cannot be responsible.

SUBSCRIBERS failing to receive
their paper promptly and regularly
will confer a favor by reporting the
fact at once.

WE INVITE FARMERS to write us
on any agricultural topic. We are
always pleased to receive practical
articles. Rejected matter will be returned on receipt of postage.

No anonymous communications or
enquiries will receive attention.

Address THE SOUTHERN PLANTER,
RICHMOND, VA.

ENTERED AT THE POST-OFFICE
AT RICHMOND, VA., AS SECOND-
CLASS MAIL MATTER.

TO ADVERTISERS.

Please bear in mind that we must have all copy or instruc-tions for advertisements by the 25th of each month without fail. Every month we are compelled to omit advertising in large volumes for the simple reason that copy does not reach us in time.

A NEAT BINDER.

If you will send 30 cents to our Business Office, we will send you a neat binder made of substantial Bristol Board, in which you can preserve an entire volume or one year of the Southern Planter. Many of our readers find these a useful device, as they always save their copies for reference.

WITH THE ADVERTISERS.

The Batemen Mfg. Co. has several advertisements in this issue describ-ing its celebrated "Iron Age" tools.

The Nickel Plate Fence Co. is a new advertiser this month. Look up the ad.

The Sumter Telephone Mfg. Co. has an announcement in another column which will interest our readers.

The Kalamazoo Stove Co. starts the season's advertising this month.

Cabbage plants in countless num-bers and endless varieties are offered by D. Q. Towles.

The M. Campbell Co. has an impor-tant announcement regarding its in-cubator on another page.

The Lovejoy Co. resumes its adver-tising this month.

A splendid cattle stanchion is offer-ed by Bowen & Quick. See their ad.

Among the largest shippers of cab-bage plants in the South is C. M. Gib-son. See his card on another page.

The Dixie Mfg. Co. advertises a very unique novelty in the shape of a match box. Look up its ad.

W. F. Allen, the strawberry speci-alist, starts the season's advertising this month.

Attention is invited to the adver-tisement of Tuttle's Elixir, to be found on another page.

The Blue Ridge Berkshire Farm is another new advertiser this month. Their offering consists of Royally-Bred Berkshires.

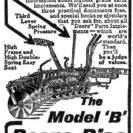

Poultrymen will be interested in the advertisement of R. S. Showalter.

Finely-bred Shorthorn cattle are offered by Dr. D. M. Kipps.

Truckers will be interested in the advertisement of the Champion Potato Machinery Co., to be found on another page.

Materals for home mixing of fertilizer can be had of the Coe-Mortimer Co. Look up its announcement in this issue.

Shorthorn fanciers will be interested in the announcement of Mr. R. R. Smith in another column.

Ballard & Lanham, Inc., the well-known Washington Real Estate men, are offering exceedingly desirable farms this month.

The Rex Guano Distributor is offered by John Blue. Farmers are invited to investigate the merits of this machine.

Berkshires of rare good breeding are offered by P. H. Gold.

"Modern Silage Methods" is the title of a very valuable book issued by the Silver Mfg. Co. Refer to its advertisement and send for a copy, which will cost you postage only.

ST. NICHOLAS

For Boys and Girls.

is the best magazine in the world, and a veritable treasure house of entertainment for all ages from three to eighteen—providing something to read to the children of three to five, wholesome amusement for the youngsters a little older, and splendid stories for the girls and boys of twelve to eighteen.

John Hay once said: "I do not know any publication wherein a bright-minded child can get so much profit without the possibility of harm as in its fascinating pages."

St. Nicholas is a splendid investment. The coming year of St. Nicholas will include a new story by the popular author of "The Crimson Sweater;" a new serial, by the author of "Fritzi;" Gen. O. O. Howard's stories of famous Indian chiefs he has fought and known; a series of illustrated humorous verses, "The Happychaps," by Carolyn Wells, and scores of other good things.

The special departments, For Very Little Folk, Nature and Science, the St. Nicholas League, The Riddle-Box, and Hints and Helps for "Mother," will be bigger and better than ever.

Can you afford not to subscribe for St. Nicholas? Only $3.00 a year. Send for special Christmas offer.

The Century Company, Union Square, New York.

THE WAY IT'S DONE.

"Mother, may I get in the swim?"
"Yes, my darling daughter.
Buy your gowns from a Frenchy store,
And don't wear half you oughter."
—Lippincott's.

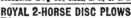

A neat Binder for your back numbers can be had for 30 cents. Address our Business Department.

ELMWOOD NURSERIES.

Attention is called to the advertisement of J. B. Watkins & Bro., Midlothian, Va., Proprietors of above-named nurseries. This firm is among the best known nurserymen in the South and grows, in large quantities, practically every sort of tree, vine or shrub that is worth while. A postal will bring you the latest catalogue. You will find it interesting and valuable.

FOR COLD ROOMS HARD TO HEAT.

The coming of the cold weather gives rise to the question of how best to heat those rooms and hallways of the house that seldom, if ever, warm up, no matter how big a fire there may be in the furnace or other heating apparatus.

The best way out of the difficulty is the use of auxiliary stoves—and of these it would be difficult indeed to find anything so handy and at the same time so clean and economical as the Perfection Oil Heater.

To begin with, it is absolutely safe. The wick can be turned as high or as low as possible without danger. But perhaps the most desirable feature of all is its convenience. The Perfection Oil Heater can be easily carried to any part of the house where more heat is required. It may be a cold bedroom, a chilly hallway, a sickroom. Or you can use it to heat the bathroom while you take your morning bath—then dress by it—and then carry it to the dining-room and eat your breakfast in comfort. The occasions on which it can be called into use are numerous—and once you have tried the Perfection Oil Heater you'll wonder why you ever struggled through a cold winter without one. Another advantage is the smokeless burner, which prevents any of the unpleasantness that perhaps have given you a poor idea of oil heaters in general. It is very handsome in appearance, and is beautifully finished in nickel and japan.

Another home comfort for the long winter evenings is the Rayo Lamp, which can be used in any room in the house—from parlor to bedroom. It has the latest improved burner, making it unusually safe and clean, and an ideal lamp for all around household use.

The Perfection Oil Heater and the Rayo Lamp, combining as they do to make the house warm and cheerful, are valuable additions to any home, and no household should be without them. They are sold at a moderate price by dealers everywhere.

Bedford Co., Va., Aug. 22, '07.
I have learned a great deal from the Southern Planter in the last year, which I appreciate very much.
      H. M. THOMAS.

Tell the advertiser where you saw his ad.

A FARM LEVEL.

The Bostrom-Brady Manufacturing Company, Atlanta, Ga., is advertising a farm level which, it seems to us, every farmer should own. Most of us get an engineer if we have any draining or ditching to do. This expense of $10 to $15 per day can be dispensed with if one of these levels is owned. Look up the ad and write for circulars and prices.

TORNADO ENSILAGE CUTTERS.

We recently examined a specimen of shredded fodder just as it came from the Tornado Ensilage Cutter. We do not hesitate to pronounce it excellent and edible to the last particle. We have had a great many complaints recently about animals refusing to eat shredded fodder or that after eating it the animals mouths became sore. Seeing the above sample, only emphasizes our contention that if the ensilage is properly shredded, not only will the animals eat it all, but with no bad after effects. The moral of this brief note is, investigate the merits of the "Tornado" by writing W. R. Harrison & Co., Massillon, Ohio, for catalogues and particular. See their ad.

REAL ESTATE HERALD.

This is the title of the catalogue issued by Pyle & Co., real estate agents, Petersburg, Va. A large number of desirable farms, located in Southside Virginia, are listed. This company would be delighted to mail a copy to any interested party. Look up the advertisement.

BLUE RIDGE BERKSHIRES.

The attention of Southern Planter readers is called to the new advertisement in this number of the Blue Ridge Berkshire Farms.

This is an age of specializing, and these farms are occupied solely in the production of the greatest Berkshire types. Heading their herd is Lord Premier of the Blue Ridge, 103555, one of the greatest boars in America. Look up the advertisement.

BARRED ROCKS AND LEGHORNS.

Plymouth Rock and Brown Leghorn breeders will be interested in the advertisement of Mr. C. C. Wine, Mount Sidney, Va. His Plymouth Rocks have that narrow barring so much sought after. His S. C. Brown Leghorns are the best he ever raised. Mr. Wine reports a greatly increased business, and if you want a cockerel you will do well to get in your order early.

OVERBROOK OFFERINGS.

The Overbrook Farm offers this month a couple of registered Angus heifers in calf to a Prince Ito bull. Many of our readers will recall the fact that Prince Ito, sold for $9,100, and was a champion of champions.

Please Mention the Southern Planter.

MOLASSES AS STOCK FOOD.

The feeding of molasses to horses and cattle has received the attention of many breeders and feeders of late years. It has not come into that general use its merits deserve. Having had many inquiries of late as to where molasses could be procured, we induced Mr. J. S. Biesecker, 59 Murray Street, New York, to offer it through our advertising columns. In his advertisement he offers to send free a booklet entitled "Molasses, a Food for Horses and Cattle." Sit down now and drop him a postal for it. You will find that it contains a great deal of information. Better give him your name for his new catalogue, too, if you are interested in purveying or producing milk or butter.

GOLD MEDALS FOR DEERE & CO.

Eleven gold medals have just been awarded to Deere & Co. for their exhibit at the Jamestown Exposition.
This company erected their own building on the exposition grounds, and being the only building of the kind there, was headquarters for every one interested in either buying or selling farm machinery.
Deere & Co. have been awarded medals at every world's fair or exposition of national or international importance since 1867.

GOLD MEDAL AWARDED TO THE SUCCESS MANURE SPREADER.

The old reliable Success Manure Spreader has just received another addition to its long list of honors. This time it is a testimonial from the Norfolk Exposition.
The manufacturers, the Kemp & Burpee Manufacturing Company, Syracuse, N. Y., have just received official notification that the Success Spreader has been awarded a gold medal by the Norfolk jury of awards.
The award is just bestowed. The Success Spreader, formerly called the Improved Kemp Spreader, was the first really successful spreader manufactured. Among the many late comers it has continued to hold its own. It has made its way into all the States, and the yearly sales, instead of being lessened by reason of its many late competitors, are actually on the increase. This is simply a recognition by the farmers of the country, and emphasized by the Norfolk award, that the Success Spreader is a machine well nigh perfectly adapted for the handling of manure.
We congratulate the Kemp & Burpee people on the honor. Their machine has already been of incalculable benefit to farmers. The more Success Spreaders that find their way on to farms the better it will be for this country's soil and crops.

Burke Co., N. C., Aug, 1907.
I could not do without the Southern Planter, or I would not want to do without it. A. H. CONLEY.

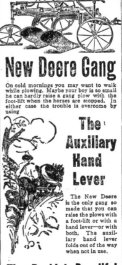

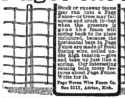

GOOD HOUSEKEEPING.

MRS. BENEDICT'S CAKE.

One and a half cups of brown sugar, half cup of lard and butter mixed, the yolks of 3 eggs, 3 cups of flour, 1 cup of sour milk, 1 teaspoon of soda; half teaspoon each of cinnamon, cloves and mace; half pound of seeded raisins, one dozen walnuts chopped, but not too fine. Bake in a loaf and ice. It will keep fresh a long time and is one of the best cakes we ever tried.

PLAIN CAKE.

The whites of 3 eggs and 3 whole eggs, 1 cup of butter, 4 cups of flour, 2 cups of sugar, 1¼ cups of cold water, 1 teaspoon of soda and 2 of cream tartar. Season with almond. Bake in layers. Filling—Two cups of sugar, 1 cup of new milk. Boil until it thickens, stirring all the time. Spread quickly on the cake.

GINGER SNAPS—VERY GOOD.

Three quarts of flour, 2 cups of lard, 1 heaping teaspoon of soda, 1 teaspoon of salt, 3 tablespoons of ginger, 3 tablespoons of cinnamon, half teaspoon of cloves, 1 teaspoon of salt, 2 cups of brown sugar, 1 egg beaten in a half cup of sweet milk. Mix the flour, soda, salt and spices together and then rub in the lard; mix well and add the egg beaten in the milk. Then mix to a stiff dough with molasses, roll thin and cut in small shapes.

COCOANUT CANDY.

Put 6 cups of sugar in a pan with a cup and a half of water and let it boil until it threads, when a spoon is dipped into it. Then take it off and beat hard for some minutes and pour over 4 cups of grated cocoanut, beat a few minutes longer and spread on buttered dishes. When partly cold mark off in blocks to make it break regularly.

WALNUT CANDY.

Six cups of brown sugar, 1 cup of milk, 2 cups of walnut meats, 1 teaspoon of butter. Stir all the time it is cooking and just before it is done add the walnuts, or just after you take it off. Beat it until it begins to stiffen then pour into buttered dishes.

NESSELRODE PUDDING.

One can of pineapple, 1 pound of candied cherries, half pound of pecans, half pound of blanched almonds; all cut into small pieces and pour over the mass two cups of good sherry; let it stand all night. In the morning take 2 quarts of rich cream and 2 quarts of custard, freeze to a mush, then stir in the fruit and nuts and let it stand packed in the freezer for several hours. Serve with this sauce: The yolks of 8 eggs beaten to a cream with 8 tablespoons of powdered sugar. Stir over the fire until it just begins to thicken. Take it off and beat until cold, then add a cup of rum and stir in a quart of whipped cream.

PINEAPPLE TAPIOCA.

One cup of tapioca, 1 cup of sugar, 3 cans of pineapple, 2 lemons. Pour 3 cups of boiling water on the tapioca and cook it until it is clear. Remove from the fire and add the juice of the lemons, the sugar and the pineapple. Put on ice or in a cold place and eat very cold with cream.

CARAVEN.

OLD VIRGINIA'S ENTERPRISE.

While the year just closed has been one of marked enterprise and progressiveness, it is extremely doubtful if any State in the Union has made greater strides in that respect than old Virginia. In no field of endeavor is this more consistently illustrated than in the live stock and agricultural industries of this State.

Undoubtedly the most influential movement for improving the live stock interests of Virginia inaugurated the past year was the organization of a company for that particular purpose. This organization is styled "The Virginia Stock Farm Company, Inc.," and has its principal office and establishment at Bellevue, Bedford County, Va. In reality, this company is a "State Live Stock Improvement Society," as it is formed for the purpose of improving the live stock in Virginia by propogating and having for general distribution at reasonable prices standard types of the particular breeds best adapted to the practical purposes of the farmers and stockmen of Virginia. This company is organized and incorporated with an authorized capital of $100,000. The officers and directors are experienced breeders of influence, several of them being gentlemen of national reputation, while all are exceptionally well qualified for the offices they hold, as may be seen from the following: President, Col. James P. Woods, Roanoke, Va.; Vice-President, Hon. Henry Fairfax, Aldie, Loudoun County, Va.; Secretary, Edward C. Burks, Bedford City, Va.; Treasurer, John Victor, Lynchburg, Va.; General Manager, J. Elliott Hall Bellevue, Va.; Corporation Counsel, Hon. J. Lawrence Campbell, Bedford City, Va. The Board of Directors consists of the following gentlemen: Col. James P. Woods, Roanoke, Va.; Hon. Henry Fairfax, Aldie, Loudoun County, Va.; Gen. John B. Castleman, "Castlewood," Louisville, Ky.; Dr. J. G. Ferneyhough, D. V. M., B. S., State Veterinarian, Burkeville, Va.; James McCollister, "The Oaks," Circleville, Ohio; Hugh N. Dyer, Roanoke, Va.; Dr. S. B. Hartman, "Hartman Farm," Columbus, Ohio; F. H. LaBaume, Agricultural and Industrial Agent Norfolk and Western Railroad, Roanoke, Va.; J. Elliott Hall, "Trace View," Bellevue, Va.; J. J. Scott, Bedford City, Va.; C. G. Smith, Roanoke, Va., and Edward C. Burks, Bedford City, Va. From the Board of Directors there was elected an Executive Committee

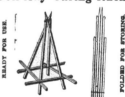
A neat Binder for your back numbers can be had for 30 cents. Address our Business Department.

of five members, as follows: F. H. LaBaume, Roanoke, Va.; Hugh N. Dyer, Roanoke, Va.; J. Elliott Hall, Bellevue, Va.; J. J. Scott, Bedford City, Va.; Edward C. Burks, Bedford City, Va. The "list of stockholders" is growing rapidly and contains some of the most prominent breeders in America.

The company has purchased a large stock farm in the eastern portion of Bedford County, near Bellevue, comprising about 830 acres, upon which is located a fine old colonial mansion, which will be the residence of the general manager. The cost of this property was $30,000. It is the intention of the company to purchase adjacent lands from time to time until they acquire 5,000 acres, all of which will be devoted to raising standard types of pure-bred live stock.

The system of operating the company's establishment is very complete. A separate "department" will be established for each breed. The "departments," which are first in importance and establishment, are those devoted to propagating standard types of the following breeds: Percheron horses, Shorthorn cattle, Dorset sheep and Poland-China swine. In addition to these there will be "departments" not so completely established at the beginning. One of these will be devoted to breeding heavy harness horses of the standard type. Hackneys will be the breed used most extensively, although a few of the more desirable specimens of the American trotter may be given a trial later on. The American saddle horse will be alloted a "department," as he is undoubtedly as useful and necessary to the farmers and stockmen of Virginia as any breed of horses. A "department" will also be reserved for the thoroughbred, his purpose being to propagate a class of stallions suitable to sire heavy-weight hunters—the sort that bring the long prices on the Eastern markes. Attention will also be given to mule raising. All mares that do not fill the requirements of a given standard will be relegated to the "department" devoted to the production of this useful hybrid.

As time goes on and the demands increase, the field of operations will be extended. If found necessary or believed advisable, other breeds will be introduced from time to time as the circumstances may warrant. However, it is generally believed that the above named breeds will fully meet the requirements of the Virginia farmers and stockmen and that the present policy of the company, as herewith outlined, will be sufficient to accomplish the purpose of its inaugurators and be of untold benefit to the breeders of the entire country, and those of Virginia in particular, should stand ready and willing to aid and support this organization in any manner they can, that the new year may be a successful and happy one for the stockmen of the Old Dominion.

THE MARRIAGE QUESTION.

ALICE WINSTON.

Of all the questions that perplex the public to-day there is none of such vital importance as that of marriage. There is a desire in all for happiness and a belief that in marriage we may expect it. In that state we look for a devotion which never changes, a trust which never fails and the satisfying companionship of kindred souls.

"O human love, thou spirit given
On earth of all we hope in Heaven."

Yet the newspapers ring with tirades from married people to the effect that marriage is a failure, and with replies from old maids that it is a success. As it is an institution which cannot be abolished—for it is ordained of God—it would be well to see where the fault lies, if it be not with the people who enter into it rashly or from wrong motives rather than with the state itself. The deep interest taken in the question calls for a health commission to find out the causes of the evil. As there is no poison without its antidote, we may hope a remedy will be found before the subject is shelved.

That it fails to give changeless and unalloyed happiness even to those who have a solid foundation of pure and unselfish love and thorough esteem cannot be denied. The monopoly of bliss will be broken by little jars and disappointments which do not materially cloud the sunshine of a true marriage.

But it must be something more than little jars and disappointments which cause so many people to declare marriage is a failure. Let us see why constitutes the majority of the unhappy ones and why they say it is a failure.

There are the mercenary marriages. "All for money" is their motto. If they get it they have what they wanted and ought to be silent. Love, honor, good temper and intelligence were not mentioned in the bond. Their case can be dismissed without further hearing.

There is the romantic marriage. "All for love and the world well lost" when the solemn vows are not taken "soberly and advisedly" but with as little thought as if it were an engagement to dance the german. A man meets a pretty, smiling girl at a summer resort. He has a nice moustache and a good figure and makes love charmingly. They become engaged and marry, each thinking the other perfection. Alas! the belief in perfection only exists in the unmarried. They are ignorant of each other's tastes, habits and dispositions. When the disillusion and rebound comes it is apt to shipwreck their lives, unless there is great good sense on one side or the other and great forbearance. Five cases out of ten the man finds he has for a life companion an ill-

tempered dunce, whose idea of industry is to crochet a tidy with a parrot on it. She has no soul above the cut of a dress and her only idea of religion is to have a new bonnet Easter Sunday. He has a sneer at matrimony always on his tongue and says it is a failure. Or the girl who may be of a high and noble nature finds she is mated to a good-looking animal without brains, honor or energy. She says in bitterness of spirit marriage is a failure, whereas the failure is in her want of reflection and deliberation. There is a spirited determination in young people to do their own marrying, to listen to no advice and tolerate no opposition, however rational. There is so much blind folly and perversity on the subject that I would advise any girl with a shady past and weakly health who is trying to ensnare an eligible young man to stop being attentive to his mother, sending her flowers and going to hear her favorite preacher. Insult all his relations, boast of the deadly diseases in the family, rake up the dreadful scandals about mother, aunts and sisters. The young man's relations will, of course, comment unfavorably upon her. He at once constitutes himself her champion, says he will not be dictated to, and to prove he is a free agent marries her. When he finds he has a sickly, uncongenial wife and a lot of ricketty children, an ill-managed home, he says with a sigh, "marriage is a failure."

If a worthless man wants a wife let him select the purest, most generous-hearted, refined girl of his acquaintance. Let him demonstrate his drunkenness, his laziness before her father, who will resent that such a man should aspire to his daughter. He speaks sternly of the young man's faults and as plainly as he can he points out the objections to him. The lover comes, admits it all, and says only her influence can save him. There is a passion for missionary work and a thirst for martyrdom in the tender female heart. She will save him, as if any woman can successfully rival the whiskey bottle! In the years of bitter trial, when she is old before her time, when love and hope are dead, she blames matrimony instead of recognizing that it was her own self-will and disobedience, disguised as self-sacrificing constancy, which ruined her life.

It is of importance that there should be good health in the contracting parties. No one with incurable hereditary taints ought to marry and entail in the future generation a life hideous with disease and deformity or clouded with insanity or maddened with drink. There is an outcry about the rights of this or that. Criminals, dogs and donkeys all have their rights insisted upon, but there is no recognition of the rights of unborn children. It is a mock modesty or deadly selfishness which ignores

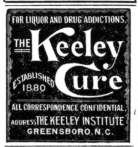

them. Oliver Wendell Holmes says each of us is the casting up of a long column of ancestors. Yes, each of us, for the poorest and plainest have the same antiquity of descent as the "Four Hundred," although it may be less honorably known. Better that column should stop when there is scrofula, catalepsy, deformity, madness, kleptomania, lying, cowardice, laziness and idiocy to be added up.

Dinah Mulock Craik, one of the most sensible women, who made the world better by living in it, says, after a long examination, she found that married life in France was more harmonious and affectionate than in England. There was more regard for domestic ties, and it was no uncommon sight to find three generations living together in peace and happiness. I am aware that the words "French marriage" will straightway bring up an idea of infidelity and immorality with many worthy people. But if their system is shown to be both moral and happy in its working, it would be well to adopt it as far as it can be made to suit our race—at least the parents ought to be allowed a vote in the matter. American parents are famous for their devotion to their children, yet from some silly idea of respecting the freedom of the latter, they refrain from having a voice in the most important event of their children's lives. If the word "French" is objectionable we can substitute "royal marriage" in its place, for I do not see that unions among crowned heads, with all "the fierce light that beats upon the throne," are shown to be as unhappy as those of many private individuals who only consulted their own inclinations. At any rate, we do not hear either from royalty or from France the mournful cry that "marriage is a failure."

FUN FOR THE BOY.

The parents of a Baltimore lad, a pupil in one of the public schools, are fond of boasting that their hopeful has never missed a day's attendance at school during a period of eleven years.

On one occasion the proud father was asked to explain how this apparently impossible feat had been accomplished. "Did he have the usual childish diseases — measles, whooping cough, and son?" the father was asked.

"Oh, yes."

"How, then, could he have always been at school?"

"The fact is," explained the father, "he has always had 'em during the holidays."—Harper's Weekly.

DIFFERENT PACKAGE.

"Roper says he always buys his cigars by the box."

"I don't believe it."

"Why?"

"That stuff is sold by the bale."—Lippincott's.

A BEAUTIFUL VIRGINIA HOME

Located only 25 miles from Washington, 2 miles from steam station; contains 295 acres, 260 acres cleared, balance in fine timber The land is under a very high state of cultivation; well fenced with best wire fencing; watered by excellent streams and wells. The soil, which is a dark loam with red clay subsoil, is especially adapted to grain and grass. The dwelling contains 12 rooms, bath, hot and cold water, and wide porches; is situated on a high elevation, giving an excellent view of the mountains and surrounding country; dwelling is surrounded by a beautiful lawn shaded by massive oaks. There are ample barns and outbuildings for farm needs, all in good condition There are five acres in fine young orchard and a large old orchard of apples; 60 acres seeded grain.

We are authorized to offer this beautiful home and excellent farm, with all modern farm machinery, 300 barrels of corn, about 40 tons of hay and straw, 6 fine horses, 25 head of good cattle, 60 sheep, 50 fine hogs, and to give immediate possession, for an extremely low price, with easy terms. This is one of the finest farms of the size in Loudoun County, and is a genuine commercial proposition as well as one of the most beautiful homes in this section. Write us to-day for fuller description, or come to see us and let us show you this fine farm.

BALLARD & LANHAM (Inc.),
621 Thirteenth Street, N. W.,
Washington, D. C.

Tell the advertiser where you saw his advertisement.

OUR DISAPPEARING FORESTS.

The position which the United States has held as a lumber-producing nation has, perhaps, been due more to white pine than to any other wood. The timber of this valuable tree which has played a most important part in the material devlopment of the nation is fast disappearing and now it is as costly as the finest American hardwoods.

Rev. Edward Everett Hale, the chaplain of the Senate, who has al ways taken an interest in forestry, deplores the passing of white pine as our foremost wood, and tells how in his own lifetime he has seen the day when "the masts of every vessel that sailed the Seven Seas were made from New England-grown pine! while to-day very little white pine is cut in New England big enough to furnish a good-sized spar." He tells, also, to illustrate the increasing cost of the wood, that he ordered a set of book shelves on which the cabinet-maker made a price, and then asked whether they should be of mahogany or white pine.

The white pine production has shifted from New England to the Lake States, and Michigan was the leading lumber-producing State for twenty years, from 1870 to 1890, with a supremacy based on white pine. In these two decades the cut was one hundred and sixty billions of board feet, valued, at the point of production, at not less than two billion dollars, or nearly half as much again as the value derived from all the gold fields of California from from their discovery in the late forties until the present. The rich forests of Michigan were once thought inexhaustible and lumbering continued in a most reckless manner for years. Suddenly the people awoke to the fact that the thoughtless destruction of the trees had thrown six millions of acres on the delinquent tax list. These white pine barrens point to the terrible penalty of wasting the forest resources which should have been the heritage of all future generations.

An idea of the increasing scarcity of white pine timber is given by the New York F. O. B. quotations, on a basis of carload lots. "Uppers" of the best grade, cost $97 to $114 a thousand board feet, and the "selects" or next lower grade cost $79.50 to $99.50. Men who are not yet middle-aged remember the time when these grades could be purchased at $15 to $25 a thousand feet. The present quotations on quartered white oak, which are $75 to $80, offer another basis of comparison which indicates the condition of the market for white pine.

The best stands of this timber now in this country are in scattered sections in Minnesota, New England, and Idaho. The species in Idaho is sometimes called silver pine. Some of the country's best white pine is found on the Indian reservations in

Minnesota and Wisconsin and scattered stands are found in the States of Wyoming, Montana, Colorado, and one or two other States. At the present rate of cutting, the tree will soon be practically a thing of the past. The small stands in the National forests are inconsiderable, but they will be managed with the greatest conservatism by the Government through the Forest Service, and through this method and practice of reforestation it may be hoped that the fine old tree will furnish timber for other generations.

LEAKY ROOFS.

With the facilities that are at hand nowadays for the prompt, economical and substantial repairing of roofs, there is less excuse than ever for the man who neglects this work.

No matter what kind of roof you have, a very little money spent for a good waterproof coating, and a few minutes or hours of your time, as the case may be, will make any leaky building on your place as snug and watertight as ever.

There is a material called Elastica Liquid Roof Coating that may be applied to shingle, tin, iron, slate, tile or any other sort of roofs, which is giving satisfaction wherever used, and which may be had in small or large quantities at a very reasonable price.

This Elastica is absolutely waterproof and is applied as easily as paint, though it has four times the body of paint. It sticks and stays wherever applied, and has saved hundreds of people the cost of a new roof or expensive, troublesome repairs.

It is made and sold direct to the consumer by Geo. Callahan & Co., 129 Front St., New York. This firm has manufactured roofing materials for 20 years, they sell to the U. S. Government, railroads, factories and mills, as well as to individuals. They know what their coating will do and they guarantee it to give satisfaction or money will be refunded.

Write this company at the above address and request their free booklet. This booklet not only describes their Elastica Roof Coating and their Rubber Cement, but gives clear and valuable instructions on how to locate leaks in all kinds of roofs. They will be glad to send this booklet promptly to any of our readers.

FOR POTATO GROWERS.

Every potato grower knows about Aspinwall Potato Machinery. It is known to be of the highest grade. Whether you have decided to buy new machinery or not, you owe it to yourself to write for 1908 catalogue. It gives valuable information and full description of the latest potato planters, cutters, sorters and sprayers. See advertisement in this number of Planter. You will do the Planter a favor to mention it, in writing for above catalogue.

FEDERAL AID TO THE IMPROVEMENT OF HIGHWAYS.

Report and Resolutions Submitted by the Committee on Public Highways of the National Grange, at Its Annual Meeting, November 12-21, 1907, and Unanimously Adopted.

Your Committee on Public Highways has had under consideration, not only the broad question involved in the improvement of the public highways, but it has given special attention to the plans of the Executive and Legislative Committee to make the Grange campaign, in favor of Federal aid, effective. That plan is approved by the Committee and the large amount of work already accomplished, in preparation of a vigorous campaign in support of the Grange plan, is in the highest degree commendable and reflects great credit on our Executive and Legislative Committee, who have perfected arrangements to bring to secure the enactment of the necessary legislation by Congress, the aid of the large industrial, commercial and manufacturing interests of the country.

In addition to this, arrangements are perfected to prosecute the campaign vigorously among the farmers in all unorganized sections of the country and through farm organizations not affiliated with the Grange.

The plans are so perfect and comprehensive that a vigorous prosecution of the campaign all along the line is assured, and one that we may feel confident will bring early success.

Your Committee, therefore, unanimously approve the recommendations of the Worthy Master and the Executive Committee.

The resolutions referred to this Committee are in harmony with the plan and are hereby approved and incorporated in the following—which, if approved, will become the platform, as it were, on which the Grange campaign will be fought:

Whereas, The improvement of the highways of the country is a matter of general public concern, and should properly receive the attention and assistance of the National Government, and

Whereas, The revenue by taxes paid by the people of the country as a whole should be devoted as far as possible to purposes which will benefit the greater number of the taxpayers in all sections of the country, and

Whereas, No argument can be advanced in favor of the annual appropriations by Congress on behalf of river and harbor improvements that does not apply even more strongly to the improvement of our public roads; therefore,

Resolved, That the National Grange favors a general policy of good roads construction by the various municipalities, counties and States, and

Resolved, That we favor the imme-

diate enactment of legislation by Congress making liberal Federal appropriations for the improvement of the public highways of the country, these appropriations to be expended in such manner as Congress may prescribe.

Arrangements are made for giving these resolutions wide circulation in the press and in circular form. We therefore ask your unanimous endorsement.

Fraternally submitted,
COMMITTEE ON PUBLIC HIGHWAYS,
Oliver Wilson, Chairman.

Extract from the Address Delivered by Ex-Governor Bachelder, Master of the National Grange, at the Annual Convention of That Body, November 12-21, 1907.

Federal Aid to Improvement of Public Highways.

At the last annual meeting, you endorsed the recommendation made in my address that the Grange inaugurate a campaign of education, having for its object the enactment of legislation by Congress providing for a Federal appropriation of $50,000,000, to be divided into five annual appropriations of $10,000,000 each, to be expended for the improvement of the public highways. These recommendations not only received your endorsement, but you instructed your Legislative Committee to take the necessary steps to inaugurate such a campaign.

Since the last meeting, your Executive and Legislative Committe have given close attention to the work of preparing for this campaign, and we are confident that the time has now arrived when the movement should be prosecuted vigorously, with the view of securing the necessary legislation at the present session of Congress, if possible. This, your Legislative Committee, has made every preparation to do, and I recommend that you take such action before you adjourn as will show that it has the united support of the order in this important matter. The demands of the Grange are both reasonable and just, and we may expect prompt action on the part of Congress if members of the order generally impress their Senators and Representatives with the fact that they are in earnest. The roads of the United States have too long been a reproach and byword among the nations. The Grange is determined that this must be ended, and we should not cease in our efforts until the Federal, State and Municipal Governments are co-operating in the work of making the American roads the finest in the world.

We invite the co-operation and support of every farmers' organization in the South in this campaign for Federal aid in making good roads. Good roads will help more farmers than will be helped by improving the navigable rivers and harbors for which so much

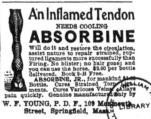

money is being asked and expended. It is is no use making rivers navigable if the farmers cannot get their products to them. Write your Senators and Representatives to help the good roads movement.—Ed.

BOOK OF "BUSTERS" FREE.

If you want to learn all about an invention that many planters claim is the greatest labor saver and money maker since the Cotton Gin, send a postal card to Henry F. Blont, 1405 Main St., Evansville, Indiana, and by return mail he will send you—free—the Book of "Busters." This book gives full information regarding the wonderful Blount's "True Blue" Middle Breaker or "Buster" and is filled with letters from some of the best known and most sucessful planters of the South, in which they tell their own experiences with this remarkable implement.

No matter what kind of soil you have to deal with—no matter how many kinds of "Busters" you may have tried without success, Blount's "True Blue" certainly do the work and do it right, at less cost in time, men and mules than you ever thought possible. They are not only fine for plowing up old stalks and bedding land, but for cultivating. They are very compact, with short beams, enabling you to plow clear to the end of the row.

The experience of men who have been using them for several years proves that they materially increase the yield, besides the saving of time and labor.

C. H. Teal, of Colfax, Alabama, writes:

"They are very satisfactory for the following reasons: Their beams are short, and can for that reason make smaller turn rows and ditch banks. They are of very superior steel and last well. The parts are made with such care that any one can put in the new pieces without even the use of a file. I have plows of yours that I have been using seventeen or eighteen years, and nothing remains of the original plow but the beam and frog. They take the ground readily. I am using more than one hundred of them, and would not change for any other make now."

Write to Mr. Blount today and get the free book by return mail.

BOG SPAVIN.

Chas. E. West, Gotebo, Okla., writes Nov. 15, 1097, "I am in receipt of your letter of recent date, I purchased your ABSORBINE from the druggist and applied it according to directions as given for Bog Spavin and had grand success. One bottle was enough to do the work.

I can give high praise for your ABSORBINE and shall recommend it for Bog Spavin above all other medicines that I tried, and I tried a good many

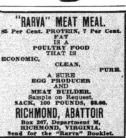

"Don't You Know"

that I do not have any sympathy for a man who has nothing but "scrub" stock around him? Especially when he could have the best **Draft Horses, Milk, Butter and Beef Cattle** and the **Finest Hogs,** if he would only come to the

LYNWOOD STOCK FARM

and select a Stallion and some Mares, a Bull and some Cows and a Boar and some Sows.

Do not put the matter off any longer; the longer you delay, the longer you will be out of pocket the big dividends that such stock always pay when properly handled. It takes no more food and time to feed an animal that will pay you large profits than one that cannot be sold for cost of raising.

JOHN F. LEWIS,
Lynnwood, Rockingham County, Va.

STONEWALL JACKSON 4995.

Probably the handsomest specimen of the Morgan family in existence. An old picture of Godolphin Arabian, to whom all Morgan horses trace through Justin Morgan, is a striking likeness of him, in pose, conformation and especially of a peculiar crest, ear and hind leg and abnormal distance from eye to ear. This stallion is naturally gaited also has the straight trot of the harness horse. Will make the season of 1908 at BUFFALO STOCK FARM, Greene County. For pedigree, terms, keep of mares, etc., address
E. T. EARLY, AMICUS, VA.
Not responsible for accidents.

Capt. J. A. Early, Doylesville, Va., writes December 2, 1907: "I am in my 82nd year; have seen and raised many fine horses, but my son's colt by Stonewall Jackson is the finest in size and form I ever saw."

Bargains in Horses.

A splendid pair of work Mule Colts, coming 2 years old. Extra fine; large as ordinary 3 year old; drives nicely to a buggy or light wagon. Will be sold at a bargain.

One 7-year-old Dark Bay Mare, 15 hands; weight about 1,000; compact and easy to keep. A reliable worker everywhere and a capital Brood Mare.

One splendid 2-year-old Sorrel Gelding; drives nicely, single and double; very compactly built. Will make a splendid family or work horse.

These horses are perfectly sound and will be sold at a bargain to the quick purchaser.

W. M. WATKINS & SON,
Saxe, Charlotte County, Va.

CHANTILLY FARM

HIGGINBOTHAM BROS.

FAIRFAX, VIRGINIA.

BREEDERS OF GAITED SADDLE HORSES AND HUNTERS.

Please mention The Southern Planter.

---

different kinds. I remain as ever your customer."

ABSORBINE penetrates to the seat of trouble promptly and effectually, without blistering or removing the hair. Does not require the horse to be laid up. Mild in its action but positive in its results. It will give you satisfaction. $2.00 a bottle at druggist. Mfg. by W. F. Young, P. D. F., 109 Monmouth St., Springfield, Mass.

THE COMPANION AS A NEW YEAR'S GIFT.

Nobody is too young, nobody is too old, to enjoy reading the Youth's Companion. For that reason it makes one of the most appropriate of New Year's gifts—one of the few whose actual worth far outweighs the cost. Welcome as the paper may be to the casual reader on the train, at the office, in the public library, it is, after all, the paper of the home. The regularity and frequency of its visits, the cordial sincerity of its tone, make for it soon the place of a familiar friend in the house. Like a good friend, too, it stands always for those traits and qualities which are typified in the ideal home, and are the sources of a nation's health and true prosperity. Is there another Christmas present costing so little that equals it?

On receipt of $1.75, the yearly subscription price, the publishers send to the new subscriber the Four-Leaf Hanging Calendar for 1908 in full color.

Full illustrated Announcement of the new volume will be sent with sample copies of the paper to any address free.

THE YOUTH'S COMPANION.
144 Berkeley Street,   Boston, Mass.

"SURE HATCH" PRIZES.

The Sure Hatch Incubator Company announces a Prize Contest for the year 1908 which will far exceed in liberality all previous contests.

The Company has divided the United States into six districts and increased the number of "hatching" prizes in each district to seven, making 42 prizes, besides numerous cash prizes for the best photographs showing the "Sure Hatch" Incubator in operation.

The majority of the prizes are "Sure Hatch" Incubators, which are well worth striving for, as these incubators are famous the world over for their splendid hatching qualities.

The Sure Hatch Incubator Company is the largest incubator concern in the world, and sells its output direct from factory to user at the factory price, on unlimited trial.

Readers of this paper who are interested in raising poultry for profit should write to the Sure Hatch Company, Box 8, Fremont, Neb., or Dept. 8, Indianapolis, Ind., for the "Prize Circular" and valuable book on incubators and Poultry Profits, both of which are free, postpaid.

THE SUN.

(Baltimore, Md.)

Now sells for 1 cent, and can be had of every dealer, agent or newsboy at that price.

All subscribers in District of Columbia, Virginia, North and South Carolina, Pennsylvania, Delaware and throughout the United States can get the Sun by mail at 1 cent a copy.

The Sun at one cent is the cheapest high-class paper in the United States.

The Sun's special correspondents throughout the United States, as well as in Europe, China, South Africa, the Phillipines, Porto Rico, Cuba and in every other part of the world, make it the greatest newspaper that can be printed.

Its Washington and New York bureaus are among the best in the United States, and give the Sun's readers the earliest information upon all important events in the legislative and financial centers of the country.

The farmer's paper. The Sun's market reports and commercial columns are complete and reliable, and put the farmer, the merchant and the broker in touch with the markets of Baltimore, Norfolk, Charleston, New York, Chicago, Philadelphia and all other important points in the United States and other countries. All of which the reader gets for one cent.

The woman's paper. The Sun is the best type of a newspaper morally and intellectually. In addition to the news of the day, it publishes the best features that can be presented, such as fashion articles and miscellaneous writings from men and women of note and prominence. It is an educator of the highest character, constantly stimulating to noble ideals in individual and national life.

The Sun is published on Sunday as well as every other day of the week.

By mail the Daily Sun, $3 a year; including the Sunday Sun, $4. The Sunday Sun alone, $1 a year.

Address

A. S. ABELL COMPANY,
Publishers and Proprietors,
BALTIMORE, MD.

At a term of the circuit court in Ohio not so long ago a "horse case" was on trial, and a well-known "horseman" was called as a witness.

"Well, sir, you saw this horse?" asked counsel for the defendant.

"Yes, sir, I—"

"What did you do?"

" I just opened his mouth to find out how old he was; an' I says to him, I says, 'Old sport, I guess you're pretty good yet.'"

At this juncture counsel for opposing side entered a violent objection. "Stop!" he cried. "Your Honor, I object to any conversation carried on between the witness and the horse when the plaintiff was not present!"

Harper's Weekly.

PATTERNS BY MARTHA DEAN.
Southern Planter patterns are designed by Martha Dean, and are up-to-
date in every way and selected each
month from the latest season's patterns. All seams allowed for. Full
directions, including quantity of material, accompany each pattern. In
ordering, be sure to give number and
size of pattern wanted. For ladies'
upper garments, give bust measure;
for skirt and under garments, give
waist measure; for misses and children, give age and size. Bear this in
mind. Price, 10 cents each. Address
Pattern Department, Southern Planter, Richmond, Virginia.

A Graceful Frock for the Tiny Child.

Although Fashion seems to have de-
creed that the wee ones shall wear
washable dresses at all seasons, manifestly in order that the freshness and
daintiness of their garments may always be assured, many mothers sensibly dress their small children with
due regard for the weather conditions.
The pretty little frock sketched is
suitable for development in either
silk, wool or linen, though it was
modelled, as shown, in a soft, washable woolen fabric, with hand embroidery in white silk for the decoration,
narrow frills of lace finishing the neck
and sleeves. The embroidery might
be omitted, however, and ribbon or
silk braid substituted for it. The
shaping of the dress is very simple,
the skirt portion being set in gathers
into the yoke, which is cut square in
the back and in front is shaped pret-
tily to correspond with the wide box
plait that ornaments the front of the
frock. The sleeves may be made
short or of full length, as the season
may demand. For the 2-year size,
2 1-4 yards of 27-inch goods will be
needed.
4252.—Sizes: ½, 1, 2, 3, 4, 5 years.
The price of this pattern is 10 cents.

A Graceful Walking Skirt.

The present season has produced no
more attractive skirt than the 7-
gored, tuck-plaited model displayed in
the accompanying drawing. It pos-
sesses, too, the rather uncommon advantage of being equally becoming to
slender or stout figures. The effect of
combined smartness and elegance is

achieved largely by the arrangement of the plait, a graduated triple box plait ornamenting both front and back, while two groups of tuck plaits appear between. The plaits are stitched in position over the hips, and below are permitted to hang in free, well-creased folds. The wide hem is finished simply with a double row of stitching. As illustrated, the skirt is cut to round length and made of navy blue panama, but the pattern may be adjusted to either short, round or instep length, if desired; while it may be developed with admirable effect in taffeta, brilliantine, or serge. For the medium size, 6 yards of 44-inch material will be needed.

6958.—In seven sizes, from 20 to 32 inches waist measure.

The price of this pattern is 10 cents.

A Pretty Comfort Gown.

It is during cool weather that one realizes the indispensibleness of a dainty morning gown which may be slipped on during the day at any time when ease is desired. Here is sketched a gown in challis, having broad yokebands and front trimming band of plain material to contrast. The gown is one well liked by particular women and is found to be easily made and becoming. The waist may be girdled with a soft ribbon or a shaped belt of the trimming fabric, the front of the gown being full and the back fitted by gores. The medium size calls for 9 yards of 36-inch material.

6901.—Six sizes, 32 to 42 inches bust measure.

The price of this pattern is 10 cents.

A Charming Design for a Dressing Sack.

A dainty dressing sack is a truly feminine garment, and finds many devotees during every season of the year. A charming design for one in mull or lawn with bands of coarse lace inset is sketched and will please the woman who fashions her own clothes. The sack is trim at waist and neck so that none of that negligee appearance is evident, while the deep collar and elbow sleeves are most becoming. The sack is one suitable to development in a tub fabric, silk or

cloth, and requires little labor to make. For the medium size, 3¾ yards of material 36 inches wide are needed.
6919.—Six sizes, 32 to 42 inches bust measure.

The price of this pattern is 10 cents.

SPAVIN AND RINGBONE.

There is a prevalent belief that if the lameness attending bone spavin or ringbone is not relieved by firing, nothing more can be done to effect a cure. This theory, however, does not hold good according to the claims made by Fleming Bros. who have advertised in this paper for a number of years. They guarantee to refund the cost of their Spavin and Ringbone Paste if it fails to cure the lameness, and there are no restrictions whatever. They say that when treated by their method, the old cases that have been fired unsuccessfully are practically as certain to yield as the recent ones. Fleming's Vest Pocket Veterinary Adviser, a book of 129 pages, is sent free to interested persons. Address Fleming Bros., No. 280 Union Stock Yards, Chicago. Ill.

AMBIGUOUS.

A Washington correspondent who used to run a newspaper in Iowa tells how the heavy advertiser of the town once entered the editorial offices and, with anger and disgust depicted in every line of his face, exclaimed:

"That's a fine break you people have made in my ad. this week!"

"What's the trouble," asked the editor in a tone calculated to mollify the indignant one.

"Read it and see!" commanded the advertiser, thrusting a copy of the paper in the editor's face.

The latter read: "If you want to have a fit wear Blank's shoes."—Harper's Weekly.

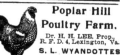

TAYLOR'S
White Wyandottes

Again gave proof of their quality by winning at the Virginia State Fair. First Pen Hens, second Hen, second Pen Pullets, first and third Pullet. I will sell a quartet, 1 Cockerel and 3 Pullets, late hatched Wyandottes, at $4. Fine Utility Cocks at $1.50 and $2. Let me know your wants and the prices you wish to pay; can supply you, but write soon, as stock is going fast.

Won at Jamestown Exhibition second Drake, second Duck, White Pekin Ducks. First Drake, first Duck, White Muscovy Ducks. Eggs in season, $3.50 per 12. First Drake, first Duck Alesbury Ducks. Eggs in season, $3 per 12. White Pekin Duck Eggs in season, $2 per 12.

R. RANDOLPH TAYLOR,
Hickory Bottom Poultry Farm, Negrofoot, Va.

R. F. D. No. 2, Beaver Dam, Va.

OUR WINNINGS

AT THE VIRGINIA STATE FAIR, Richmond, Va., October 7-12, 1907, were
First pen Partridge Wyandotes.
First pen Partridge Wyandottes.
First pen S. C. Rhode Island Reds.
(The only three pens we showed.)

Spring Hatched
COCKERELS
and
PULLETS
of the above breeds.
FINELY BRED,
VIGOROUS STOCK.
Write for prices.

ELLERSON POULTRY YARDS,
J. W. Quarles, Prop., Ellerson, Va.

Here is a Bargain.

An extra fine lot of Cockerels and Pullets in White Wyandotte (Duston strain), White Orpington (Cook), and Barred Plymouth Rock (Bradley Bros.) at reasonable prices. Prize winning and utility birds. Also fine Mammoth Bronze Turkeys. Perfect beauties. Write now, while they are here, to MISS CLARA L. SMITH,
Landor Poultry Yards, Croxton, Caroline County, Va.

S. and R. C. R. I. Reds, White Wyandottes, S. C. B. Leghorns and B. P. Rocks. Eggs for hatching $1 for 15; $1.75 for 30; $2.75 for 50; $5 for 100. All breeding stock mated; S. and R. C. Red stock. RIVERSIDE POULTRY FARMS,
J. B. Coffman & Sons, Props., Dayton, Va.

PURE-BRED
BRONZE TURKEYS
Mammoth in size, correct in plumage. The quality of our birds is unusually fine this year. The price remains the same—Hens, $3; Toms, $5. If you don't like them better than ours do your money they are ours and your money back.
W. G. HUNDLEY, Dog and Chicken Fancier, Callands, Va.

N. B.—Many wrote us last year after we had sold out. You, reader, may be one. We undertook to answer every inquiry personally but found we could not. We again solicit your orders.

A Neat Binder for your back numbers can be had for 30 cents. Address our Business Department.

WASHINGTON NOTES.
Good Roads Work.

The good roads microbe has multiplied rapidly in New York. The State appropriated $5,000,000 last year out of money realized from the sale of an issue of fifty million dollars worth of bonds authorized by an amendment to the State constitution. This is going some. For this good road construction the State pays one-half the cost, the counties 35 per cent. and the township or property owners 15 per cent. The bonds run for fifty years and pay three and a half per cent. interest. An annual tax of .0055 mill upon each dollar's worth of property for every million dollars worth of bonds outstanding is provided to pay the interest and create a sinking fund with which to redeem one-half the bonds. The rest of the bonds are to paid in fifty equal annual installments by the county and townships wherein the proceeds have been applied to the improvement of highways. The result is that New York promises to become the Good Roads State of the Union, even vyeing with Massachusetts, where miles and miles of splendid State boulevards have been constructed within the past few years. The old days of the farmers plowing up the sides of the road and throwing the sod into the middle, when there is no work upon the farm that can be done, and thus working out the road tax, promises to become a thing of the past in the Empire State, or at least relegated to the remote corners.

School of Farriery.

Last month Colorado inaugurated a new school of applied science—that of farriery or horseshoeing. This is according to E. H. Mullen, a Denver veterinarian, who was in Washington the other day. The new school has the backing of the horseshoers' union of Denver, and the indications are that the course, which is to be of five months' duration, will be exceedingly popular. The foot is certainly one of the most important parts of the horse.

The blacksmith who shoes the horse, Mr. Mullen said, has it in his power to either ruin the horse or make it a valuable and long-service animal. It is necessary that the farrier knows what he is about when he attempts to nail a shoe to the horse's foot. He must be familiar with the horse's foot and have a general knowledge of the anatomy of the animal. As far as I know we have no school in America where this is taught to any but veterinarians. We propose to make it a part of our course at our Agricultural College with the idea that we will enable our farmers and stockmen to understand how the horse's foot should be shod and cared for, and those who desire to embark professionally in the business can here gain the foundation which, with practical experience, will enable them to do scientific work. The course will be very practical. We have but few text books and the students will be taught by lectures and practical demonstration in the shop. The consruction and anatomy of the foot will be explained and students will be taught how to make shoes and fit them. Denver horseshoers are among the most scientific workers at the trade in the world, and they became so by educating themselves in the very things that are proposed in the new course at Fort Colins. It is astonishing how little horsemen know about the feet of their animals. Most of them seem to think that any one can nail on a shoe and that that is all there is to it. More horses, I believe, are ruined by faulty shoeing than in any other manner.

From some government investigations in apple growing now in progress, it appears that it is going to be possible to produce annual crops on varieties of apples which are accustomed to bear only in alternate years.

War on the Cattle Tick.

Co-operation is assisting largely in the control of Texas Fever, which, it is estimated, costs the country in the neighborhood of $50,000,000 annually. At the Conference held at Nashville, Tennessee, at which representatives of the Bureau of Animal Industry and State authorities interested in the extermination of cattle ticks took part, the attitude of the Bureau toward the subject was outlined by Chief A. D. Melvin, and notes on the co-operative work thus far carried on were presented by R. P. Steddom. Such work has been done in nearly all the Southern States, as the gravity of the problem is fully recognized. During the first year of co-operative effort, about 550,-000head of cattle have been inspected, and an area of 50,000 square miles has been apparently freed from ticks and released from quarantine. This means a great boon to this territory and the results encourage the belief that with an annual appropriation of $250,000 the cattle tick can be ultimately eradicated.

It is held that tick eradication is practicable and may be accomplished by a system of rotation of pastures, by the starvation plan, by picking or brushing ticks from the cattle, and by oiling. It is recommended that cattle be examined weekly, beginning about October 15th, and treating with crude oil so long as any ticks are found. Under ordinary conditions, a thorough application in October, will make it unnecessary to give further treatment until March. The oil may be applied with a brush or with a piece of burlap, and all parts of the cow should be covered.

Tuberculosis in Cattle and Hogs.

The Bureau of Animal Industry has made a number of tests showing that the most important factor in the spread of cattle tuberculosis is the manure. It has been generally supposed that milk was not likely to be affected unless the cow's udder was tuberculous. The Bureau has found, however, that the manure from diseased cows is usually heavily laden with tuberculous bacteria and as these are easily and almost surely introduced into the milk, under ordinary methods of milking, a single tuberculous cow may affect the milk of an entire stable.

Hogs Infected from Cows.

Hogs, according to the Bureau, also easily acquire tuberculosis from following cows in the pasture, or from feeding on skim milk or separator milk from tuberculous cattle. The great increase of tuberculosis among hogs is stated by the Bureau of Animal Industry to be almost entirely, traceable to their association with affected cattle, and the Bureau strongly recommends the sterilization of all skim or separated milk from public creameries before it is fed to calves or pigs. Tuberculosis among animals is not necessarily acquired through the mouth, nose or respiratory organs, as has been generally supposed. For instance, tuberculosis of the lungs was produced in hogs by inoculating them in the tips of their tails.

Human and Animal Tuberculosis.

There has been considerable dispute as to whether human and bovine tuberculosis are practically one and the same, the famous Koch theory raising a storm of dissension—at least as to whether human tuberculosis or consumption can result from the consumption of tuberculous milk, etc. Dr. Melvin, Chief of the Bureau of Animal Industry, holds to the view that the two forms cannot be classed as separate and distinct diseases and that measures to protect persons from infection from tuberculosis from animals are highly necessary. "But whether," he said, in speaking of the matter, "the subject is regarded from the standpoint of protecting human health or of promoting the welfare of the live stock industry, it is beyond question or argument that it is highly important for our stock raisers, farmers and dairymen to eliminate tuberculosis from their herds.

Dr. Melvin's predecessor as Chief of the Bureau of Animal Industry, D. E. Salmon, also held that bovine tuberculosis was transmitted to humans, and he took the very sensible view that even admitting there was doubt about the matter, the only safe course to pursue was to assume that it was transmissible and to make and enforce regulations accordingly.

Forest Preservation.

The sermons on forest preservation and conservation which are being preached by the Government Service are bringing good results. At least there is continuous work along the

lines suggested. For instance, the
Cleveland Cliffs Iron Co. is beginning
to re-forest a portion of its lands in
the upper Peninsula of Michigan.
Preparations are being made to re-
plant next spring with pine and hard
woods nearly 15,000 acres of the large
area owned by the Company, and, if
this plantation succeeds, to continue
the work. There is no reason why it
should not succeed, if properly under-
taken. A present undesirable characteristic of much of Michigan and Minnesota, as well as other States, is the
vast extent of cut over timber land,
with only stumps to show. This land,
had it been rationally timbered, as
the Forest Service would say, should
now have a vigorous second growth,
but it was cut by men who had no
thought of the future; only the maximum gain at the time of cutting.
When these forests were cut, timber
was ample; it was simply a question
of filling contracts and getting the logs
down when the water ran. Now lumber is scarce; in fact, about double
in price than it was when we were
ten years younger. If, in the succeed-
ing ten years, it should again double,
we would better build the chicken
house of brick or cement. Neverthe-
less, wood must always play an important part in farm work. We cannot
get along without it. The action of
this Company—which owns some
1,000,000 acres of cut-over lands—is
commendable and, if followed out by
every other timber holder, would materially ameliorate the impending lumber famine. It will pay to look into
the profits from timber planting. It
is claimed that it pays now to plant
trees. If lumber doubles in price in
the next decade, those who plant trees
now should have a fairly safe investment.

If our roads were sufficiently improved, generally, so that the average
load of wheat hauled, which is now,
according to Government statistics,
fifty-five bushels, could be increased
to seventy-five bushels, the saving ef-
fected to the farmer, in hauling our
annual crop from the farm to the railroad, would be between $6,000,000 and
$8,000,000.

GUY ELLIOTT MITCHELL.

KNOX'S JOKE.

One day last spring Senator Knox
was walking through a corridor of the
Capitol, when he was joined by a
former member of the Senate, Mr.
Chandler, of New Hampshire.

As the two drew near the entrance
to the chamber, Mr. Knox motioned
to his companion to pass in first.

"After you," said Mr. Chandler,
with a polite bow, drawing back.

'Not at all," protested Knox; "the
X's always go before the Y's (wise),
you know."—Harper's Weekly.

Pittsylvania Co., Va., Sept. 23, '07.
I like the Southern Planter very
much. J. W. NEAL.

Nash Co., N. C., Sept 11, '07.
I find I cannot get along without the Southern Planter.
R. T. GRIFFIN.

Appomattox Co., Va., July 31, '07.
I think the Southern Planter is the best farm paper I have ever read.
REV. G. W. LEWIS.

WANT ADS.

tories and land should rapidly enhance in value. Adjoining farms, without railroad frontage, can't be had for the price asked for this per acre. Snap as an investment. Price, to a quick purchaser, $1,700. Will stand a loan of $900. Address D. B. Prosser, Atlanta, Ga.

FOR EXCHANGE—BLOCK OF STOCK in factory earning about 15 per cent. Purchaser can probably have position at about $20 per week. Want Southern farm. S., care Southern Planter.

WANTED—TO TRADE STOCK OF A lumber and coal company in State of Washington for Virginia farm; par value stock $5, trade on $2.50 basis; trade up to 20,000 shares. Address Box 155, Fayette City, Pa.

FOR SALE ON THE SOUTH CAROlina coast, Morgan Island, 400 acres highland and extensive marsh range seven miles. Created specially for a horse ranch. C. S. Johnson, Beaufort, S. C. Lock Box 161.

CHEAP CORN, COTTON, RICE AND Timber Land for sale. Robert Hill, Des Arc, Ark.

WANTED—CHEAP SOUTH CAROLINA plantation. E., care Southern Planter.

LIVE STOCK.

HOLSTEINS FOR SALE—TO AVOID inbreeding, I offer for sale to a quick buyer, the richly-bred bull, Netherland Clethilde Monk's Count, a very fine individual, as well as a richly-bred one; very quiet and kind. Also have a Bull Calf by him out of Maggie Clethilde, which I will sell at farmers' prices. Its dam is now giving six gallons a day. Born on October 1, 1907. William W. Jackson, Bizarre Dairy Farm, Farmville, Va.

FOR SALE—TWO REGISTERED Ayrshire Bulls; one two years old, price $45; one two months old, price $15. Dr. William Crawford Johnson, Frederick, Md.

NICE LOT OF BERKSHIRES ABOUT three months old; also Boars ready for service; Sows safe in pig. Evergreen Farms, W. B. Gates, Proprietor, Rice Depot, Va.

FOR SALE—TWO FINE HOLSTEIN Bull Calves; richly bred; good as the best; $35 and $25. William R. Lewis, Route No. 1, Blackstone, Va.

REGISTERED DUROC SWINE; THE most prolific hog bred. Choice Pedigreed Pigs for sale at farmers' prices. Clarence Shenk, Luray, Va.

FOR SALE OR EXCHANGE FOR Jersey Heifers of equal breeding, Registered Galloway Bull, 3 years old, A1. W. S. Mott, Dixondale, Va.

PURE-BRED BERKSHIRE PIGS, Collie Puppies and Shorthorn Calves for sale at low prices. Thomas H. McGechin, Greenwood, Del.

SEVERAL PONIES, SHETLANDS AND Grade, 42 to 49 inches; gentle for children. John M. Cunningham, Brandy Station, Va.

TRY LARGE YORKSHIRE HOGS— You will wish no better. W. E. Stickley, Strasburg, Va.

REGISTERED BERKSHIRES, BLUE ribbon quality. Write us your wants. Fairfield Farm, Nokesville, Va.

PRIZE HOLSTEINS, JERSEY RED and Chester White Pigs and Roofing

Slate cheap. W. M. Benninger, Benninger, Pa.

FOR SALE—PURE-BRED SHORThorns—three cows, Calf and 15-months Bull. N. Boush, Clarksville, Va.

POULTRY, ETC.

FOR SALE AT A BARGAIN,—BEING overcrowded, will sell at less than half cost price, 43 Pure-Bred R. I. Reds, Yearling Hens and 5 Cockerels; 20 High-Bred White P. Rock Yearling Hens, 4 Cocks; one Charles A. Cyphers 140-Egg Incubator; 3 Cyphers & Co., 140-egg each. Any these at $10 each. Also 2 Incubators holding 900 eggs each, 450 eggs each side; can be run separate apartments; also 390-Egg Incubator. All being used only one year. Will exchange for S. C. W. Leghorn Pullets and Yearling Hens; pure-bred stock only. Aldress Belport Poultry Farm, P. O. Box 15, Portsmouth, Va.

PURE-BRED WHITE WYANDOTTES for sale. Having recently bought Fall Creek Poultry Farm, will dispose of all poultry, consisting of over 600 White Wyandotte Pullets and Cockerels; all pure-bred and splendid healthy stock; Pullets, $1; Cockerels, $1.50. Also three Sure-Hatch Incubators and Brooders. John Kubovec, R. F. D. 1, Ashland, Va.

FOR SALE—BUFF LEGHORN AND White Wyandotte breeding stock; exceptional quality; also large Imperial Pekins, Northern strain. Address J. B. Watts, Pulaski, Va.

WANTED—PURE-BRED MAMMOTH Bronze Turkeys, Toms and Hens of early 1907 hatch and older; state age, what quantity and price. H. H. Meschendorf, Forest Depot, Va.

SILVER LACED WYANDOTTES— Several of my finest breeding Cockerels for sale yet. Will satisfy critical buyers. Prices right. Write today. S. P. Yoder, Denbigh, Va.

LEGHORNS, WHITE AND BROWN; Silver Spangled Hamburgs, Indian Runner Ducks. Quality unsurpassed; hardy. Stock and Eggs for sale. Fairfield Farm, Nokesville, Va.

WHITE HOLLAND TURKEYS—A FEW first-class Hens and Toms for sale or will exchange hens for different strain. Mrs Helen Briesmaster, Sabot, Va.

ROSE COMB RHODE ISLAND REDS— A few choice Cockerels for sale, $1.50 to $2 each. Miss Louise V. Spencer. Blackstone, Va.

WHITE HOLLAND TURKEYS—OLD Toms, $4, young Toms $3, Hens $2.50, trios, $7. B. L. Hill, Bumpass, Va., R. F. D. No. 2.

FOR SALE—LARGE MUSCOVY Ducks, very hardy and most prolific variety. W. B. Coleman, Mannboro, Va.

SIX WHITE PLYMOUTH ROCK Cockerels, one Cock, 1 each. Eggs in season. Addie Cowherd, Gordonsville, Va.

FOR SALE—PURE-BRED PEKIN Drakes, Rhode Island Reds. Mrs. Armstrong, Union Mills, Fluvanna County, Va.

PURE-BRED RHODE ISLAND RED Cockerels, $1 to $2 each. Address Elmwood Poultry Farm, Pinetown, N. C.

FOR SALE—A FEW WHITE HOLland Toms from $2.50 to $3.50 each. G. W. Moss, Guiney, Va.

POSITIONS—HELP.

POULTRYMAN WITH LIFE EXPErience in all branches desires position on salary or salary and percentage of profits; experienced at dairy work; five years with last employer; small family; good habits and an every-day careful worker. Address, with full particulars, York State Poultryman, care Southern Planter.

YOUNG MAN WHO DESIRES TO learn business wants position with some one in the poultry business for next year. Address R. T. Conway, Holliday, Va.

WANTED—BY EXPERIENCED MAN, position as working farm manager for next year to begin first of January. References exchanged. Manager, care Southern Planter.

MAN HAVING FARM WISHES PARTner of practical experience and some capital in cattle business or dairy farm and hog raising. Address Box 196, Charlottesville, Va.

MISCELLANEOUS.

A VALUABLE BOOK—DO NOT FAIL to write now for copy. Ideal Hand-Book, 144 pages useful information for shooters. Send 3 stamps for mailing. We will also send following catalogs upon receipt of postage: Rifles, 5 cents; Revolvers, 2 cents; Gun Sights, 2 cents. Morrisette Repeating Arms Co., Mail Order Department, Box 240 S. P., Richmond, Va.

WANTED—TO BUY ALL KINDS Wild Birds and Animals, particularly Tame Deer, Wild Turkeys, White Squirrels, Peafowl, Otters, Red Foxes, Grey Squirrels, Partridges, Pheasants, Beaver. State price when writing. Dr. Cecil French, Naturalist, Washington, D. C.

FOR SALE—ORCHARD GRASS SEED, grown in Fauquier County, Va.; acclimated; guaranteed free of ox-eye and first-class in every respect. Prices and samples gladly furnished on request. Address McGill & Son, The Plains, Va.

CABBAGE PLANTS FOR SALE— About half a million fine Cabbage Plants for sale at $1.50 per 1,000; lots of 5,000, $1.25 per 1,000; 10,000, $1 per 1,000; leading Varieties. R. F. Du-Vernet, Sunnyside Truck Farm, Greenville, S. C.

DO YOU KNOW A CHILD WHOM you wish to make happy for a whole year? "The Little Folks' Magazine" will bring joy to the little ones; between the ages 4 and 12 years; 12 times a year, only $1. Single copies, 12 cents. Robert A. Morrisette, Mail Order House. Magazine Subscription Department, Box 240 S. P., Richmond, Va.

FOR EXCHANGE—CHAMPION SELF-Rake Reaper for small gasoline engine or iron lathe. Address L. K. H., care Southern Planter.

Yadkin Co., N. C., Aug. 2, '07·

I think the Southern Planter is the best farm paper published in the South, and I must have it.

S. W. GARNER.

Norfolk Co., Va., July 31, '07·

I like the Southern Planter so well I want to have all the numbers.

G. ELLINGSON.

A TRYING SITUATION.

Adhering too closely to an isolated fact, or condition, may result in misfortune, if not disaster.

Missouri Hines, a citizen of Wyoming, commonly called M'Zoo Hines for short, once recounted to friends an experience which befell him while in camp for the night on Western plains.

"I was due to lay out for sure," said he, "an' I didn't have no fuel of any kind. So I makes my fire of grass —just set my coffee pot and fry pan on a bunch of it—and starts in to cook supper comfortable. Fire sort of begun to edge off along the grass, me followin' with my fry pan. The wind come up like, and the fire started to travelin' right quick, me followin' all the time and just holdin' my fry pan over the edge of the blaze—."

"Did you get the bacon cooked, M'Zoo?" asked a friend. "Yes," said Mr. Hines, "but by the time it was done I found I was fifteen miles from my coffee pot."

A NORTHERN PAPER ON SOUTHERN PROSPECTS.

(From the Berkshire (Mass.) Eagle.)

Active railroad construction is going on in Virginia and a degree of mystery attends it. That the best of material is being used in the work, and that there appears to be no lack of financial backing, is apparently the extent of public information.

Sections of the State not already traversed by the extensive system of the Norfolk and Western railroad, and by other lines, will be brought into ready communication with the rest of the country. Hundreds of thousands of acres of the finest grazing and farming lands in the world are there awaiting the skill and industry of cattle men and farmers. There is already a conspicuous movement in that direction. These lands can be bought for ten dollars an acre or less.

Quite a contrast with the two or three hundred dollars an acre out in the Western corn belt.

When we consider the known high quality of the Virginia lands, that they can be bought so cheaply, that there is no more delightful all the year-round climate on earth; that more than 40 millions of the 80 millions population of the United States live within twenty hours' transportation by rail; that at Norfolk the State has the finest harbor on the Atlantic coast, we are well nigh persuaded that history is again about to repeat itself—that the Old Dominion is to become the "New Dominion"—that the Star of Empire wends its way, not westward only, but southward as well.

Instead of beef, the choicest of vegetables, California not excepted, are brought from Texas, in the winter and spring, to northern markets all along the line from New England to Colorado.

Is it too much to expect that, in the near future, we shall obtain our prime beef, and many other good things, from the Vrginias?

THEO. F. LEES.

Such expressions of opinion as the foregoing cannot fail to help us in settling up our vacant lands.—Ed.

HISTORICAL EVIDENCE.

The late Richard Mansfield was a patient sufferer in his last illness, and he retained his good cheer to a marked degree. One day he told his physician that he believed he would not live many weeks longer.

"Bosh!" said the physician. "You are good for a long time yet. Why, man alive, did you ever hear of anybody near death with legs and feet as warm as yours?"

"Yes," replied Mr. Mansfield, "lots of them. For instance, there was Joan of Arc, and the Salem witches."—Harper's Weekly.

MILITARY TITLES DISCONTINUED.

The late Senator Morgan used to enjoy telling a story illustrative of the cheapness of military titles a few years after the Civil War.

A traveller in the South was passing through a certain populous country district, and stopped to converse with a farmer who had a considerable number of men at work in his hayfields.

"Most of these men are old soldiers," said the farmer.

"You don't tell me! Were any of them officers?"

"Two of them. One there was a private, and the man beyond was a corporal, but the man beyond him was a major, and that man away over yonder was a colonel."

"Are they all good men?"

"Well," replied the farmer, "I ain't going to say anything against any man that fought for the South. That private's a first-class man, and the colonel's pretty good, too, but I've made up my mind to one thing—I ain't going to hire any brigadier-generals."—Lippincott's.

SOUTHERN HUMORISTS.
Mary Washington.
Article No. 1.

Judge Augustus Baldwin Longstreet, of Georgia, is, I believe, the earliest of our Southern humorists. He was born in Augusta, Ga., September 22, 1790. He graduated at Yale College in 1813, studied law in Connecticut, and was admitted to the bar of Georgia. In 1821 he was elected to the Legislature, and in 1822 he was made Circuit Judge. He resigned, on moving to Augusta, soon afterwards. In 1838 he entered the Methodist Episcopal ministry, and in 1839 he was made President of Emory College, Oxford, Ga. After nine years' successful administration of this office, he was called to the presidency of the Centenary College, Louisiana, and soon afterwards to the University of Mississippi. In 1857 he accepted the presidency of the South Carolina College, but returned to the University of Mississippi in 1861, and remained there until his death in 1870.

He had an extremely varied career, being by turns lawyer, judge, legislator, preacher, author, pamphleteer, educator, and president of various colleges. He is best known, however, as the author of a richly humorous work entitled "Georgia Scenes," which was published in 1840, and which enjoyed so wide a popularity that you could find a copy of it in almost every Southern home, prior to the war. A revised edition of it also appeared in 1867. Many of the characters were so racy and life-like that they became household words. Judge Longstreet afterwards wrote another humorous work entitled "Master William Mitten," but it did not possess the freshness and vigor of "Georgia Scenes."

Another of our ante-bellum humorists is Dr| George Washington Bagby, who was born in Buckingham county, Virginia, on the 13th of August, 1828, and who died in Richmond on the 29th of November, 1883. His father was a native of Lynchburg. Dr. Bagby was eucated at Princeton, N. J., and graduated in medicine from the University of Pennsylvania, after which he started to practice his profession in Lynchburg, where his father lived. He soon, however, abandoned medicine for the profession of letters. He first wrote for the "Lynchburg-Virginian," then edited by Mr. James McDonald, and many of his sketches were published in its columns; as, for instance, "The Sacred Furniture Warehouse," "Blue Eyes," and others. Early in the fifties, he and his friend, Capt. George Latham, owned and edited the "Lynchburg Express," which only ran a short time. Afterwards Dr. Bagby went to Washington City as correspondent of the "N. O. Crescent." Whilst in that city he not only wrote for "The Crescent," but for the "Charleston Mercury," "Richmond Dispatch," "Atlantic Monthly," and "Southern Literary

Messenger." It was for the last named periodical that he wrote his humorous "Letters of Moses Adams to Billy Evans of Hurdsville," which, under the guise of rustic simplicity, were filled with witty and caustic hits at people and events in Washington.

After John R. Thompson resigned the editorial chair of the Southern Literary Messenger, Dr. Bagby became one of the associate editors and continued in this position until 1864, most of his best articles having been published in that paper. In 1868 he became editor of "The Native Virginian," published at Orange Court House, and from that time on he did a good deal of lecturing in a humorous vein. His most famous lectures were on "The Virginia Gentleman," "Bacon and Greens," and "The Disease Called Love." He also delivered a lecture on fools, the tickets for which bore the following inscription: "Fools, Admit One."

Although Dr. Bagby was known chiefly as a humorist and writer of dialect stories, still he did not confine himself exclusively to this field, but essayed others, with very good success. He had, for instance, a vein of poetry in his nature, as his very good poem, "The Empty Sleeve," will attest. The fact of his having found employment with a journal of so high a standard of excellence as "The Atlantic Monthly" suffices to show that he possessed talent of no mediocre order. Physically, he was a great sufferer, so much so that it is astonishing how he could have felt sufficiently cheerful and mirthful to have played the role of humorist. It was a signal instance of the triumph of mind over matter. Physical suffering imparted to his countenance a melancholy cast at variance with the humorous bent of his mind. One who knew him well in private life says he was peculiarly kind and gentle to children, and that he was an ardent lover of his native State. Thomas Nelson Page says that his "Old Virginia Gentleman" is the most beautiful sketch of Southern life that has ever been published."

Another of our prominent old humorists was Joseph G. Baldwin, author of "Flush Times in Alabama and Mississippi." He was a native of Virginia, but moved to Alabama, where he practiced law, and from there to California, where he died, after becoming eminent in his profession. He was a brilliant and original writer, with a delightful vein of humor, strongly evinced in his book on "Flush Times in Alabama and Mississippi," dedicated to "The old folks at home—the people of the Valley of Virginia." This volume was published in 1853, and, within a year it had run into its seventh edition, which was something very remarkable and, indeed, I believe, unprecedented in those days. In a short time the characters of "Ovid Bolus, Esq.," and

"Simon Suggs, Jr.," became as well known in the South as Samuel Weller or Micky Free, and whilst the case of "Higginbotham versus Swink Slaider" became a "cause celebre." In the Southern households in the olden times, you would find this book side by side with "Georgia Scenes," and both well thumbed by both the old and young of the family. I am under the impression that Judge Baldwin also wrote another work entitled "The Partisan Leader," but this did not make a stir in the world like "Flush Times." Baldwin's biographical sketch of Seargent Smith Prentiss has been pronounced one of the finest in our language.

Mr. William Tappan Thompson, of Savannah, Ga., was another humorist contemporaneous with Baldwin. Whilst he distinguished himself in the editorial line, he is best known as the author of a grotesquely humorous work entitled "Major Jones' Courtship," which appeared in 1840. This was followed by a volume entitled "Major Jones' Sketches of Travel, Scenes, Incidents and Adventures in a Tour from Georgia to Canada."

In 1843, Mr. Thompson published a third volume entitled "Major Jones' Chronicles of Pinesville—Sketches of Georgia Scenes, Incidents and Characters." This was in the same vein as the others, but it had been worked too long, and the last volume did not win the public favor its predecessors had done.

RATEKIN'S SEED HOUSE.

HIGH-CLASS BERKSHIRES

BARON PREMIER III., 75921.

WINS AT INTERNATIONAL.

For the first time in the history of the Show, ribbons went east of the Ohio River. We are glad to further report that they came to Virginia. Mr. E. B. White, Proprietor of the Selma Stock Farm, Leesburg, Va., exhibited at the recent International at Chicago, nine head of Percheron horses and won ten ribbons, including three first, two second, three third, two fifth, and a gold medal, the latter on stallion and mares owned by the exhibitor. We had reserved space for a more extended notice of the International, but, owing to the illness of our correspondent, the manuscript did not reach us in time for this issue. However, we take pleasure in mentioning Mr. White's winning, which emphasizes the fact that Virginia has stock that will go right along with the best.

HE KNEW.

There is a well-known Federal official at Washington whose family stoutly maintain that he is absolutely color-blind, a contention as stoutly refuted by the official himself.

On one occasion at table his wife remarked a new tie her husband was wearing. "I'll wager you don't know what color the tie is," she teasingly suggested.

"It's blue," said the husband.

"Right! But how on earth did you know?"

"Well," said the husband, with the same assurance, "when I bought it yesterday I told the clerk if he didn't give me blue, I'd throw him out of the window."—Harper's Weekly.

When corresponding with our advertisers always mention Southern Planter.

KING'S IMPROVED COTTON.

This variety of cotton, which has gained such a wide reputation and which is being shipped so extensively throughout the South and more especially the boll-weevil stricken district, was grown and improved near Youngsville, Franklin county, N. C. So it has been that I have known and grown this cotton from its earliest history and my seed sold to the originator and shipped to planters throughout the cotton belt. I do not want to rob the originator of the honor of improving this cotton, but I conceived the idea soon after it was first introduced that unless some one continued to improve his cotton it would soon deteriorate by becoming mixed with other varieties but if improved in a few years the genuine King's Improved Cotton would command a much better price and at the same time the standard of the seed be maintained. This has come true, and here in this country, where the seed has been grown continuously for ten or fifteen years, the percentage of genuine seed is about 25 to 50 per cent. higher. In order to supply the demand of higher standard seed, I have neither spared trouble nor expense in growing and improving this cotton to the highest standard of perfection. It is my aim to furnish my customers with a grade of seed unsurpassed in quality and genuineness of variety anywhere. In purchasing your seed, it is very important that you deal with reliable parties, for it is often the case the planters are faked, and seedsmen are not over-zealous in trying to get the best variety.

I have given the growing and improving of this cotton much study and attention for the past ten years and have applied every means known. In order that you may know, and for the benefit of those who wish to keep their seed improved, how my seed are improved, I have printed a circular giving the information. Write me for one, also see my advertisement on another page.   I. W. MITCHELL.
Youngsville, N. C.

FARM MACHINERY HONORS AT THE NORFOLK EXPOSITION.

The Norfolk Exposition closed on the evening of November 30th last and we are now being informed as to where the honors have been placed on the various lines of modern farm machinery. Word comes of the new recognition of the excellence of a number of machines manufactured by the International Harvester Company. They received the gold medal on their Reversible Disc Harrow, Hay Tedders, Corn Shellers, Feed Mills, Manure Spreaders, Bettendorf Steel Wagons, and their new Auto Buggy. They received the silver medal on Gasoline Engines and Grain Harvesters.

Not all these machines are so well known as the mowing and harvesting machines manufactured by this Company. But in all of them the same

high standard of manufacture is maintained. The awarding of these honors at Norfolk serves to impress upon us the fact that I. H. C. machines, of whatever character, are never secondary to anything of their type that is manufactured.

The International Harvester Company also received a bronze medal for the general excellence of their exhibit.

RAISING POULTRY AS A SIDE LINE.

There is money in raising poultry for the market. As a side line, it fills in many unprofitable hours and pays handsome dividends the year round. You can start without a feather and select enough pullets from the first season's hatching to lay all the eggs you need for the next season, or you can market them as broilers at a good round price.

The business of raising poultry is one that doesn't require a large amount of money to start. For a few dollars you can buy either the Wooden Hen or the Excelsior Incubator, and either one will more than pay for itself with the first hatch. There's no need to pay high prices for incubators that won't do as well.

These incubators are made by Geo. H. Stahl, Quincy, Illinois, who is widely known as one of the largest and most successful manufacturers of hatchers and brooders in the country.

Begin to-day by writing for a free copy of Stahl's catalogue.

LOW WAGON WHEELS.

The kind of low wagon wheels that have wide metal tires with a good groove in the tire, the whole wheel made of good steel are wheels that never lose their tires when they are needed; the spokes wear much longer being protected; there is less sliding, and the wide tires improve the roads and keep the surface of the field in good condition. The low wagon is the friend of the workman as well as he team. The farmer may buy a low wagon complete or just low wheels if he will write for particulars, so as to have them fit any wagon exactly, to the Havana Metal Wheel Co., Box 6, Havana, Ill.

WOOD'S SEED CATALOGUE.

Among the interesting catalogues that reach our table, is that of T. W. Wood & Sons, Seedsmen, Richmond, Va. In addition to giving complete and accurate descriptions and illustrations of various field, garden and flower seeds, it contains full cultural directions, which the farmer will find

When corresponding with our advertisers always mention Southern Planter.

timely and valuable. This year's catalogue lists quite a number of novelties which are sure to interest all planters, large and small. This firm was awarded a gold medal at the Jamestown Exposition for general excellence of its exhibit. Be sure and write for a catalogue.

FARM AND GARDEN LABOR SAVERS.

The Planet, Jr., tools for farm and garden have an established reputation for quality as well as efficiency and they are popular everywhere. They are used successfully in Egypt and other foreign countries as they are in all sections of our own land. They represent the most advanced thought and ideas in farm implement making and hardly a year passes without the introduction of some new device or improvement to increase their usefulness to the man who tills the soil.

The No. 4 Planet, Jr., which is a combination of hill and drill seeder, wheel hoe, cultivator, furrower and plow, is the most complete tool a farmer or gardener can have on his place. With it he can do more work and keeps things in better condition with one-fourth the work required without it.

The No. 4 is only one of the many Planet, Jr. combination tools—there is one for every farm and garden task whether for hand or horse power— and all of them are sold with an ironclad guarantee of absolute satisfaction.

S. L. Allen & Co., of Philadelphia, make the Planet, Jr., tools and they issue a handsome catalogue describing them. You ought to have one of these catalogues. If you will drop a postal to S. L. Allen & Co., Box 1107X, Philadelphia, they will be pleased to send you one.

FOUTZ POULTRY REMEDY.

We call attention to the advertisement of the David E. Foutz Co., Baltimore, Md. While this Company makes numerous live stock remedies and preparations, it calls particular attention to its Poultry Remedy this month. Now is the time it can be used to great advantage. Every poultryman should look up their ad. and inquire into the merits of this remedy. This Company have been manufacturing chemists for more than fifty years and are among the very few who didn't have to revise their formulae in order to comply with the Pure Food and Drug Law.

When corresponding with our advertisers always mention Southern Planter.

SHOULD LET TREES GROW BIGGER.

Attention was lately called by Arboriculture to the way farmers rob themselves when they cut down small trees. The writer says that ten years ago he saw in Virginia about thirteen thousand apple barrels held together by hickory hoops, to make which sixty-four thousand young hickory trees had been cut down. The barrel hoops had been sold for about four hundred dollars. If the trees had been allowed to grow they would have been big enough in a few years for cutting up into carriage spokes, and would have produced at the present price of thirty-five dollars a thousand, spokes worth more than eight hundred thousand dollars. This is the kind of forestry argument that ought to appeal to owners of brush lots.

BURKE'S GARDEN, VIRGINIA.

Burke's Garden, Virginia, is Southern headquarters for the "Choice Goods." Late reports from the best Fairs and Live Stock Expositions on this continent remind us of the very close relationship between their winners and leading members of the Burke's Garden herds and flocks of cattle and sheep. This applies with special force to our leaders—Shorthorns and Hampshires.

Two of these shows in particular—viz.: Kansas City Royal and International at Chicago by setting forth animal excellence year after year, whose quality has been conceded by all foreign judges to be of superlative degree—attract world-wide attention. Anything that gets a place at either, even down to fifth, is given entre to select circles. In fact, only the choicest specimens which succeed in running the blockade of judges at county and State fairs ever get to these final round-ups. At the Royal, the Grand Championship was won by Ruberta's Goods. She is dam of the Sweepstakes cow at Richmond last year—viz.: Rubertress, from Burke's Garden. This cow—and, by the way, it is quite unusual for a calf to win sweepstakes over a long string or older first-prize winners—claims for sire a $3,500 son of Choice Goods, and half brother to Best Goods, now in use by the Burke's Garden Co. This same line of breeding—viz.: "Choice Goods"—also furnished to the International a Grand Champion in the handsome Junior Yearling, "Scotch Goods." Among distinguished matrons amongst the red, white and roans, we mention the $2,000 Golden Lassie, mother of Gondomar, first or second yearling at Iowa, Nebraska and other of the largest Western State fairs; of Good Lassie, who topped the Jones sale last June at $980; Imp. Bonnie Bella Roan, by brother to Lavinia, a Virginia-bred cow, the first to bring $2,000 this season, and daughters of Grand Champion Nominee.   W. B. DOAK.

RANDOM PHILOSOPHY.

Hate is often unconscious fascination.

The ocean roars only where it is shallow.

Titania was not the last woman to love a donkey.

Reform is a plant that grows well in the sunlight of publicity.

If friends are regarded as assets only, we will soon spend them.

Red tape is the bandage that keeps a mummified institution together.

The gossip deserves credit for choosing some one more interesting than himself to talk about.—Lippincott's.

SOME COMMON PHRASES EXPLAINED.

"Pity is akin to love." And a mighty poor relation.

"Every man has his price." Excepting always those who give themselves away.

"A complication of diseases." What a man dies of when the doctors don't know.

"Riches have wings." But the millionaires' sons usually open the cage doors.

"Ignorance is bliss." It must be, judging from the happy expressions of the majority.

"Love laughs at locksmiths." With a milliner, grocer, and ice-man, however, he is usually serious.

"Truth is stranger than fiction." Or does it only seem so because we have less chance to get well acquainted with it?—Lippincott's.

Botetourt Co., Va., Aug. 24, '07·

I am more than pleased with the Southern Planter. It is the best paper that I can find.   N. P. SIMMONS.

When corresponding with our advertisers, always mention Southern Planter.

MEASURING CORN IN CRIB—SHRINKAGE OF CORN—WEIGHT OF HAY IN MOW.

1. How many cubic feet to a barrel of cob-corn in a crib?

2. How much does corn dry out?

3. What is the weight of a barrel of corn when husked? When dried?

4. How many cubic feet of hay in a mow (each kind) after well settled to the ton?   M. A. C.

Fallston, Md.

1. A barrel of ear corn, by measure, is ten level bushel basketfuls and occuples twelve and a half cubic feet of space. An easy method of determining the barrel content of a crib is to multiply the cubical contents in feet by eight and point off two decimal places.

2. The amount of corn dried out and the weight of a barrel of corn at husking time depends upon how much moisture the corn contains. The weight of a barrel of dry corn, according to the Maryland Statutes, is 350 pounds of ear corn, or 280 pounds of shelled corn. When the corn is not dry, that is, when it contains more than 15 per cent. of moisture, enough weight should be taken to make a barrel of dry corn, the amount ranging with the percentage of moisture contained. The amount of moisture in corn at the time of husking depends upon the earliness of the variety, the wetness of the season, and the length of time allowed for the corn to cure before husking.

3. At the Kansas Station the percentage of moisture in the corn of the variety test plot varied with different varieties greatly: In 1904, from 11.90 per cent. to 29.02 per cent.; in 1905, from 11.66 per cent. to 21.86 per cent.; and in 1906, from 10.73 per cent. to 19.43 per cent. The corn was not cut until the ears were in a hard dent and then remained a couple of months in the shock before it was husked, so that it was fairly well dried out. The average per cent. of moisture was found to be about 15 per cent. The per cent. in samples of their white corn, Forsythe Favorite, one year after husking, was 12.05 per cent.

Conditions in Kansas are more favorable to well-cured corn than are the conditions in Maryland, for we usually have much more moisture, and, furthermore, corn is cut greener and not left so long in the shock as it was at the Kansas Station; hence, especially in late, wet seasons like this one, there is a much larger per cent. of moisture.

In the fall of 1905 corn from the ear row test plots of the Maryland Agricultural Experiment Station was weighed when husked and then was stored in corn racks in a steam heat-

ed class room until January 1, 1906, about two and a half months, when it was re-weighed. The Munnikhuysen corn shrank 29 per cent, in weight, and the Leaming shrank about 26 per cent. The amount of variation in percentage of moisture which different varieties may contain is shown by the variety tests at the Ohio Station, where, in a five year test, 1892-1896, the average of each variety for the five years varied from 2 per cent. with Dakota Dent to 50 per cent. with Modoc, the air dried weight being taken about April first on the average. In 1903 and 1904, the shrinkage of the varieties at the Ohio Station varied from 14.8 per cent. with the Early Huron Dent to 34.9 per cent, with the Boon County White (Tenn.), and averaged 26.3 per cent.

Percentage of shrinkage must not be confused with per cent. of moisture for corn that is air-dried still contains moisture. Hence, in comparing the data of the Kansas Station with that of the Ohio Station, or M. A. E. S., an allowance must be made for the per cent. of mosture in air-dried corn.

From these figures it may be seen that corn may be so immature at husking time that it will shrink one-half or so that 140 pounds of ear corn are required at husking time to make one bushel or seventy pounds of dry ear corn, or that it may be so well cured that seventy pounds is a bushel of corn. It is advisable to grow varieties of corn that will mature early enough so that seventy-five or eighty pounds at husking time will make a bushel of dry corn.

4. The number of cubic feet to a ton of hay in the mow varies according to the length of time the hay has settled, the depth of the hay in the mow, and the kind and quality of the hay. Alfalfa or prairie hay, which has settled a month, is usually estimated at eight feet cube, or 512 cubic feet. Where the hay has been stacked six months at seven and a half feet cube or 422 cubic feet, and when stacked a year at seven cube or 343 cubic feet.
                              C. W. NASH.

LEGUMINOUS CROP TO SEED AT
      LAST WORKING OF CORN.
Please tell me if there is any leguminous plant that I can sow at the last working of corn? German clover dies out on my bottom land.
              F. E. OMOHUNDRO.
Westmoreland Co., Va.

You can sow hairy vetch or the winter vetch in corn at the last working. If you would apply a ton of lime to the acre to the corn land before planting the corn you would no doubt succeed with the crimson clover. We know of several places where the clover would not hold until the lime had been used, and then it succeeded well.—Ed.

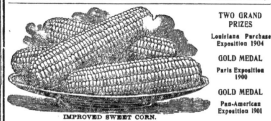

SALT MARSH MUD.

Will you kindly tell me through your columns if the mud taken from a salt marsh, and from the bed of a creek (such as I could get when the tide is out) would be of any material value. If so, how would it need to be treated for best results, and what elements of plant food would it be apt to contain.   J. H. JORDAN.

Mathews Co., Va.

We doubt much whether this mud would be of value sufficient to pay for the cost of securing it. If it had much decayed vegetable matter in it, it might be worth securing, even then, before it could be beneficially used, it would require to be weathered for a year by spreading it out to expose it to the action of the air and sun, and would need to have lime mixed with it to correct acidity. All water soaked deposits are usually strongly acid and therefore deleterious to plant growth.—Ed.

OATS AND VETCH FOR HAY.

Would like to ask—since it is too late to seed oats and vetch winter varieties, can they be successfully seeded in the spring to be cut for hay and the same land be planted to corn? If so, what time should they be seeded and when cut?   A. H. JAMES.

Lancaster Co., Va.

You can sow oats and hairy vetch in February or March and get a crop to cut for hay in May or June and follow this with corn. Sow one bushel of oats and twenty-five pounds of hairy vetch seed per acre. The hairy vetch is best seeded in the fall, but one of our subscribers tried the crop sown in February or March and made a complete success.—Ed.

FERTILIZER FOR CORN.

I have about eight acres in crimson clover that I wish to turn down for corn next spring. The land is strong enough to grow good, round Irish potatoes. Should I use fertilizer on the clover? If so, what kind and how much per acre should I use, and what time should I use it—this fall or next spring?   A. T. TIGNAL.

It would very probably help you to secure a heavier crop of corn if you applied 200 pounds of acid phosphate per acre after turning down the clover. Read the article in this issue by Dr. Stubbs, in which he explains how he is getting up his land in Gloucester county, Virginia, and securing good crops. He found his land very deficient in available phosphoric acid and we expect yours is very much in the same condition.—Ed.

SOY BEANS—ALFALFA—PUMP-KINS.

1. What will soja beans, including the vine (green weight) grow to the acre on good land cultivated in rows thirty inches a part? What propor-

When corresponding with our advertisers always mention Southern Planter.

ion of soja beans would you mix with corn in a silo? How many months or days from time of planting to maturity of soja beans, suitable for silo?

2. How would alfalfa suit as a mixture with corn to fill a silo?

3. What is the value of pumpkins or hogs?

4. How is the corn affected when he corn land is well covered with the pumpkin vines? A. D. R.
Bristol, Tenn.

1. The soy bean will, on good land, make from 10 to 12 tons to the acre of green food. Mix one-third soy beans and two-thirds corn, running them together into the silo, so that they shall be well mixed. Do not put in separate layers. They will mature sufficiently for siloing in the same time as corn, though the yield and richness of the crop will be increased by giving them a month's longer time to grow. We would plant the beans in May and the corn to be hoed with them in June.

2. Alfalfa, like the other clovers, does not make good silage. It is better to make this crop into hay.

3. Pumpkins make a good feed for hogs in the first stages of feeding, but

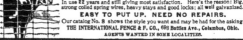

require to be supplemented with corn to harden the meat. Their great value is as an appetizer. They enable the hogs to assimilate and utilize the grain feed better.

4. Pumpkins may be grown with corn without injuriously affecting the yield. Indeed, we have subscribers who grow them regularly and claim that they get a better yield with them than without. They say that the large leaves and vines shade the ground and conserve the moisture.—Ed.

ALFALFA GROWING.

I have one acre of land that has been in a garden and potato patch for the last two years. It is rich and I want to put it in alfalfa. Please advise me whether to sow it this spring or fall? Would it pay me to sow it in cow peas this spring, and can I get two crops of them and then sow alfalfa in the fall?

I have enough horse stable manure to cover the land. How and when should it be put on? Is it best to buy seed of T. W. Wood & Son (inoculated) or will it be better to get the inoculating material from Blacksburg and inoculate the seed

W. R. PITTMAN.

Southampton Co., Va.

In your section the proper time to sow alfalfa is August. Prepare the land well this spring by ploughing deeply and breaking finely and if the land is infested with weeds keep it cultivated during the summer to kill out the weeds. Weeds are the greatest enemy to the alfalfa crop and until they are subdued you cannot expect to succeed. If the land is clean of weeds then sow cow peas and make the crop into hay in July. Then apply one ton of lime to the acre and work in with the disc harrow and let lay for a week or ten days, then apply the manure and with it 300 pounds to the acre of bone meal and again work in thoroughly with the disc or a cultivator, and having secured a fine seed bed sow the seed broadcast at the rate of 25 pounds to the acre. Either buy the inoculated seed or secure the bacteria from Blacksburg and inoculate the seed yourself, following the instructions very carefully. Harrow in the seed so as to give it a cover of two or three inches.—Ed.

PEANUT FERTILIZER.

Please send me fertilizer formula for peanuts. Our crop is short this season. S. B. E.

Surry Co., Va.

If you will refer to our issue of May last, page 441, you will find full advice on the best methods and fertilizer for growing peanuts successfully. The mere application of any particular fertilizer is not of itself sufficient to ensure a profitable crop. There should be a radical improvement of the fertility of the land brought about by the adoption of a rotation of crops

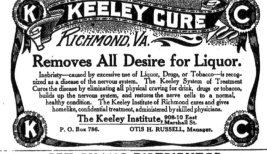

which will fill the land with vegetable matter. The best method of doing this is to grow crimson clover or vetches for a winter crop and cow peas for a summer crop, these to be ploughed down. To secure a good growth of these acid phosphate at the rate of 250 pounds to the acre should be applied and 75 pounds of muriate of potash to the acre should also be applied, as the light lands upon which this crop is grown are usually deficient in potash. Lime also is very essential to the peanut and the cow pea crop should be followed with a dressing of lime at the rate of one ton to the acre. When the lands are thus improved physically and mechanically then a proper fertilizer to use at planting the nuts is 300 pounds of cotton seed meal, 80 pounds of acid phosphate and 240 pounds of kainit or 65 pounds of muriate of potash may be used instead of the kainit.—Ed.

COW GIVING BLOODY MILK.

I have a fine cow that gives bloody milk. Can you give me a remedy? If so, what is it? Please answer in The Planter. J. D. PERKINS.
Grayson Co., Va.

Blood may escape with the milk when the udder has been injured by blows, also when it is congested or inflamed, when the circulation through it has been suddenly increased by richer and more abundant food or when the cow is under the excitement of heat. It may also result from eating acrid or irritant plants like the rannucalaceæ, resinous plants, etc. Deposits of tubercle or tumours in the udder or induration of the glands may be efficient causes, the irritation caused by milking contributing to draw the blood. The treatment will vary with the cause. In congested glands give one pound of Epsom salts and daily

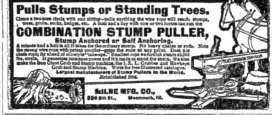

thereafter half an ounce of saltpeter with a drachm of chlorate of potash, bathe the bag with hot water and rub with camphorated lard. If the food being too rich or abundant is the cause of trouble reduce the same. If from acrid plants these must be tken out of the feed. Induration (hardening) of the udder may be overcome by rubbing with a combination of iodine ointment one part, soft soap two parts or mercurial ointment and soap may be used. Careful milking is imperative.—Ed.

MILLET SEED—CHECKING ROT IN APPLES—FLOATS—POTASH IN GRANITE.

1. I would like to know the value of millet seed as a feed for stock or poultry. Also its usual value on the market.

2. I give you my experience in saving apples that have rotten specks on them which you wish to save. Cut out the spot and fill with slacked lime. For two years I have taken some of my best culls after packing and treated them with lime in this way and they keep all right. It kills the rot and forms a dry skin or crust just like it does on a cut potato that has been limed.

3. Would also like some one to give their experience with floats or ground South Carolina rock. How long does it take to become available? What is its market value? The agents ask as much for the ground rock as they do for dissolved. How much sulphuric acid does it take to dissolve a ton?

4. I saw some time ago that the Department of Agriculture had discovered that granite stone carried a large percentage of potash and that it could be manufactured for one cent per pound. What kind of stone do they call granite? And why is it that some one is not after it?

W. F. KYGER.

Rockingham Co., Va.

1. Millet seed contains 11 per cent. of protein, 57 per cent. of carbohydrate, and 4 per cent. of fat. With these constituents it ought to be a good feed for stock, but it should never be fed unground, as it is so small that it cannot be properly ground up by the animals whilst eating it, and in this form it is indigestible. Stewart says that ground it is good feed for horses. There has been, however, much complaint that millet hay, when fed to horses with the seed in it, causes derangement of the kidneys, if is fed to hogs in the West to some extent. For poultry, it is a good feed. We cannot give market value, as it is not dealt in on this market except for seed. For this purpose the seedsmen quote it regularly.

3. In this issue, in an article by Professor Massey, you will find some remarks as to the availability of floats. If used in conjunction with

leguminous crops ploughed down, the floats become available much more quickly than has been supposed. We are strongly in favor of the use of floats for the improvement of land, as in this form the phosphoric acid is more lasting in its action and there is no risk to be run of depriving the land of its available lime content, which is sometimes the case when acid phosphate is used. The acid phosphate is more quickly available. The price of floats ought not to be so high as the acid phosphate. Nearly equal parts by weight of sulphuric acid and rock were formerly used, but now, we understand, less acid is taken than rock.

4. We have not followed closely the investigations made as to the potassic content of granite rock. We saw the report on the subject, but do not know that the process for making the potash available is being used anywhere. Granite rock is one of the oldest and hardest rock formations. We have millions of tons of it around this city, where it is utilized for building material and for paving purposes and for concrete work.—Ed.

HORSE EATING DUNG.

What is the cause of a mule or horse eating their own dung? Is there any remedy to break them of such a habit?　　　　W. M. PEARCE.
Nash Co., N. C.

The eating of the dung is usually a symptom of indigestion, which has created a depraved appetite. The

treatment for cure should be such as to remove the cause of the indigestion. Indigestion is usually caused by eating poorly cured or innutritious food, like poor hay or mouldy, heated grain. It is sometimes caused by the animal bolting its food before chewing it. There are also many other causes, as diseases of the stomach and related organs. Usually, a change to good, nutritious food fed in moderate quantities and at regular intervals will cause improvement. A cathartic ball made up of one ounce of aloes, or one pint of linseed oil should be given at the commencement of the treatment to clear out the stomach and bowels. An alkaline tonic should be given after the ball or oil has done its work. This tonic may be made up of baking soda, powdered ginger and powdered gentian, in equal parts. Mix thoroughly and give in heaping table-spoonful doses twice a day before feeding.—Ed.

BEDDING FOR STOCK—LIME FOR TOBACCO—ENRICHING FERTILIZER.

1. What is the best bedding for stock—pine tags or oak leaves?

2. Will lime be injurious to tobacco if put on the land intended for tobacco next year? The land is a grey land, with a little sand in it.

3. How much potash and ammonia must be put in a ton of 8-2-2 fertilizer to give it 5 per cent.?
STEPHEN P. POOL.

Granville Co., N. C.

1. We would prefer to use the oak leaves. Neither make the best bedding, as the pine tags are resinous and, therefore, do not readily decompose, whilst the oak leaves have a good deal of tannin in them and are slow of decomposition. Straw is preferable to either of them, as it decomposes readily and is a good absorbent of the liquid.

2. Lime applied now will not be injurious to the tobacco—used in moderation, say, not more than a ton to the acre. Used in excess, it has a tendency to make a "boney" leaf.

3. You cannot mix ammonia and potash in a mixed commercial fertilizer like an 8-2-2 brand so as to get an exact 5 per cent. content of potash and 5 per cent. of ammonia. You can add a nitrogenous fertilizer like nitrate of soda, so as to increase the ammonia, and a potassic fertilizer like muriate or potash, so as to increase the potash in the mixture, but the fertilizer will not then analyze strictly 8-5-5. If you add 200 pounds of nitrate of soda you will add thirty-eight pounds of ammonia to the mixture and one hundred pounds of muriate of potash will add forty-five pounds of potash to the mixture, and this will bring it up more nearly to the proportions you desire. As one cannot tell what were the ingredients used to make the 8-2-2 mixture, it is

impossible to apportion the quantities of them so as to know what quantity of new ingredients to add to make a strictly 8-5-5 mixture.—Ed.

A POINT OF INTEREST.

In a certain county of Arkansas a man named Walters was put on trial for stealing a watch. The evidence had been very conflicting, and, as the jury retired, the judge remarked, suavely, that if he could afford any assistance in the way of smoothing out possible difficulties he should be most happy to do so.

Eleven of the jurors had filed out of the box, but the twelfth remained; and there was on his countenance an expression indicating great perplexity.

"Is there any question you'd like to ask me before you retire?" asked his Honor, observing the juror's hesitancy.

The man's face brightened. "Yes, you Honor," he replied, eagerly. "I'd like to know, your Honor, whether the prisoner really stole the watch."—Harper's Weekly.

MERE CAUTION.

A dentist in Rochester was visited by a native of Dutchess county to be treated for an ulcerated tooth.

"That's a bad tooth," said the man of the forceps, "and I should advise you to spare yourself pain by taking gas. It will be only fifty cents more." And the dentist showed his machine to the doubtful person from Dutchess county, explaining its workings—how he would fall asleep for a minute or two and then awake with the tooth and the pain gone. At last the patient consented and took out his wallet.

"Never mind paying now," said the dentist, patronizingly.

"I wasn't thinking of paying," responded the Dutchess county person. "But I thought that if I was going to sleep I'd like to count my money first."—Harper's Weekly.

ENQUIRERS' COLUMN.

Detailed Index.

TWO MENSAHIBS (LADIES) IN INDIA.

"Traveller."

It was after a great deal of thought and the persuasion of friends who had been there before us that my friend and I decided to venture on travelling through India. At first, it seemed to us too far from home and too hazardous, but we finally came to the conclusion that no professional traveller could miss seeing India, and so we sailed away from Hong Kong for that destination. The voyage of eleven days over the tropical sea to Ceylon was a dream of loveliness, with cloudless skies, and the water as calm as a lake. At night the Southern Cross blazed forth above us and our life on ship board was as gay as Paris in the season.

We awakened from this dream to find ourselves one morning on the beach at Tuticorim, Southern India, surrounded by an army of lightly-clad coolies, and, in the hands of a solemn looking Hindu, our travelling servant, whom we called Sam, because we could not pronounce his real name. The tram was waiting to bear us Northward and Sam got our traps together, rather humiliated that we had so little, for the native Indian judges the worth of his patron by the amount of visible impedimenta he carries.

Travel in India is very hard. The heat and dust are almost unendurable, even in January, the so-called cold season. The distances are enormous, and the trains arrive and depart at the most unearthly hours. There are compartments reserved for ladies, with dressing room and servant's room attached. We got our meals at railway refreshment houses by wiring ahead for them. We often stopped at stations in the midst of the desert and found there the comforts of civilization—including ice.

The country we first traversed was a favored portion of the Empire, with sufficient rainfall to produce abundantly. There were broad fields of cotton, grain cane and rice. The landscape was pleasing. The tram followed the highway, which was shaded by a double avenue of trees, along which heavily laden camels and bullock carts plied to market. From the plain there arose many a fortressed crag, surrounded by jungles in which lurked the tiger, while around us were herds of camels, buffalo and spotted deer, troops of monkeys and brilliant tropical birds.

We passed through many villages of mud huts where the people swarmed about the station, some selling, some begging, others idling, every Pagan of them a picture in his graceful draperies. Red is the predominant note in India. It seems to suit best under those burning skies, and as the reds swayed and blended in the crowd it was gorgeous to look upon.

We broke our journey by stopping

a day at Madras, and our first ex perience with Indian habits still forms an unpleasant memory, though we had some amusement throwing shoes at the punkah-wallah to keep him awake. Such queer bugs ran up and down the dining-room walls that we ordered our meals on the gallery, where we ate them to the hissing and rattling of cobras, which snake charmers and fortune tellers brought for our amusement. The serpents spread out their heads and stuck out their tongues as their masters played to them. The chief interest of Madras lies in its connection with points of English history, and Fort St. George is full of monuments. St. Mary's church dates back to 1639, and on its memorial tablets are the names of many who helped to establish English supremacy in India. Robert Clive was married here in 1753. The name of Col. Arthur Wellesley (afterwards Duke of Wellington) appears here in the register of 1798, and his quarters can be seen from the church window. Elihu Yale, whose generous contribution to the founding of Yale University caused it to bear his name, was Governor of Madras in 1687, and was married in St. Mary's church. He contributed to it a beautiful silver alms basin, which is shown with the church plate. In the church yard are many famous names.

From this chapel we went to visit the Pagan temples. The Dravidian temples of Southern India are the chief glory of Hindoo architecture, which has neglected the home and left few other monuments. They are built with a solemn grandeur and are of enormous size and in perfect preservation. The Vimanah, or inner shrine, is built in a quadrangle, surrounded by walls, on which are high pyramidal gates or gopuram. These are covered with massive hand carvings, representing the protecting dieties of the temple. The squat figures and features of these Indian gods confront you at every turn, in their architecture, their scripture, their embroidery and arts in every form. These figures present neither beauty nor symmetry to European eyes. Various details point to a common origin of Hindoo and Mongolian art, though the museums show beautiful specimens of Greek and Persian art, which have exerted a marked influence on native arts. It is, however, to the Mogal conquerors in the North that we are to look for the most perfect and beautiful specimens of art and architecture. In Madras we were not admitted within the temples, but examined them from the outside, where the high Juggernaut's car was resting under a bamboo cover. It is carried yearly in procession through the streets, and underneath it the devout cast themselves to propitiate the god who demands human sacrifice. The most interesting of all temples to unbelievers is the one at Madara, for

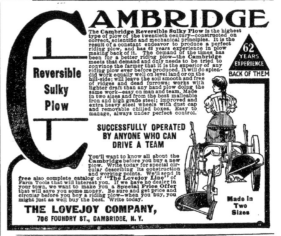

strangers are allowed access to all parts of it. It covers a parallelogram 847x729 feet, with nine gopuram, the tallest of which is 152 feet. The temple is divided into two parts—one dedicated to Minakshi, the fish-eyed goddest, consort to Siva, and the other to Siva. At the entrance is a long corridor filled with dealers and their wares, and no one moves to cast them out of the temple. We had to leave Sam here, as his caste did not permit him to enter the inner precincts. A number of priests accompanied us. In the middle of the temple is the tank of golden lillies, surrounded by a painted arcade. We came down a long, dark corridor lined with images of Hindoo saints and gods, and through rooms containing gold and silver litters into the great "hall of a thousand pillars." Though the number is exaggerated, yet the elaborate carving makes it the handsomest hall of its kind in existence. Opposite to it is the new gallery dedicated to Siva, a hall 333 feet long by 105 broad, supported by four rows of pillars. The whole temple is lighted with a "dim, religious light," half revealing, half concealing the grotesque images of kings and gods, and the effect is very weird. Its great size and noble proportions give it a dignity lacking in the other Indian temples we had visited.

During our stay here we formed the acquaintance of the Rev. James Rowland, a Tamil convert to Christianity, named for his teacher, and a member of the flourishing missionary colony of Madura. He gave us a most interesting account of his work among the natives. We had already been much impressed by the practical results of the mission work in India, where schools and hospitals are doing so much to lessen the ignorance and sufferings of the people, and even Christianity is beginning to take root a little. This is the supreme test, for many missionaries give up their lives to the cause without being able to implant Christianity in the natives, so far removed from it is the Oriental mind. and yet it is said that the Sanscrit language expresses the idea of a triune God better than any other.

Indian women have been more benefitted by the missionaries than any other class, though, alas, very much yet remains to be done before they can approach even remotely to the freedom and manifold privileges of their occidental sisters. Their condition now, however, is, on the whole, less deplorable than it was some time back, when they had no escape from the barbarous custom of child marriages, often followed either by a cruelly persecuted widowhood, or else by the scarcely worse suttee or burning on the death of their husbands. The purdah women, or those whose caste demanded their faces to be veiled, and then to be hidden behind purdahs or curtains, suffer tortures

VERY CONSIDERATE.

Mistress.—"Bridget, I hope you're not thinking at all of leaving me. I should be very lonesome without you."

Maid.—"Faith, and it's not lonely ye'll be. Most-like, I'll go whin there's a houseful o' company for luncheon or dinner."—Lippincott's.

from want of medical attention, because they could not look on any man's face or have a doctor. Women doctors are now sent out to them, and hospitals are erected by various charities for even the poor outcast, who was formerly dragged to the temple to be scourged for her soul's health if she complained of suffering.

Even to-day there is no hint nor trace of any high-caste woman to be seen abroad. We sometimes saw carriages entirely covered by draperies, in which the purdah ladies were riding, but, for the most part, they prefer being prisoners in their home and garden to this sort of airing.

CATALOGUES.

T. W. Wood & Sons, Seedsmen, Richmond, Virginia, one of the best catalogues ever issued by this well-known firm. It contains much information of value to every farmer.

Diggs & Beadles, Inc., Seedsmen, Richmond, Va. Catalogue of seeds and price list.

J. B. Watkins & Bro., Elmwood Nurseries, Midlothian, Va. Price list of fruit, ornamental trees, vines, plants, etc., for fall and spring planting.

J. S. Biesecker, 59 Murray Street, New York, Dairy and Creamery Supplies.

W. R. Harrison & Co., Massillon, Ohio, Feed and Ensilage Cutters, Blowers and Silos.

Dairymen's Supply Co., Philadelphia, Pa. Everything for the Dairy

Telephone Construction Co., Buffalo, N. Y.—The Rural Telephone.

Parke, Davis & Co., Detroit, Mich., Veterinary Notes, Vol. 1, December, 1907. This publication will be issued regularly and will be found of value to all horsemen and stock keepers. Send your name and address to the publishers and ask to have a copy sent regularly. Say you saw notice of the Journal in the Southern Planter, and you will receive it.

Ratekins Seed House, Shenandoah, Iowa. Catalogue of Farm and Garden Seeds. The largest seed house in the West.

The Johnstone Harvester Co., Batavia, N. Y. The Drop Lock Steel Stanchion for fastening cows in the stalls.

Bostrom-Brady Mfg. Co., Atlanta, Ga. Treatise on terracing, draining and ditching.

The Superior Fence Co., Cleveland, Ohio, makers of a special steel lock fence. See the advertisement in this issue.

D. Q. Towles, Young's Island, S. C., Cabbage Plant Specialist. Offers frost-proof cabbage plants.

Alfred Jouannet, Mt. Pleasant, S. C., Cabbage Plants.

Premium Lists.

Virginia Poultry Association, Richmond, Va., January 9th to 15th, 1908.

BOOKS.

Practical Farming. A plain book treatment of the soil and crop production, especially designed for the ery-day use of farmers and agricultural students. By W. F. Massey. blished by The Outing Publishing ., New York. Price, $1.50.

This is a book of 320 pages, as full information of the most valuable aracter for the farmers as an egg is 1 of meat. It is written in Professor ssey's well-known, plain, forcible nner, and is devoid of technicalis, so that even the plain, ordinary, ery-day farmer can understand it roughly and apply its teachings to daily work. It brings science down the comprehension of even those very limited education and will en le every farmer who reads and dies it to apply science in his call-. There is not a farmer in the d who cannot derive profit from ding this book and we hope to see in every farmer's home. We can pply it at the published price, but induce farmers to take and read it, will give a year's subscription to e Planter to every one who orders book from us and sends $1.50, the ce of the book alone.

The Horse Book. A practical treat on the American Horse Breeding iustry, as allied to the farm. By H .S. Johnstone, Assistant Editor the Breeders' Gazette. Published Sanders Publishing Co., Chicago. ice, $2.00 postpaid. We can supply book at this price.

In "The Horse Book," written by H. S. Johnstone, and just off the esses of the Sanders Publishing Co., whole career of the horse is ced in the plainest of language and convincing style. The author has d more practical experience with rses of all sorts than most men of years and whatever he has set wn he learned in that proverbially rd school which experience con- ots. He has sought in every page eliminate the mysterious and make in the path which those must tread o would learn about the horse. The ry is told from beginning to end in way that holds the interest of the ider, yet nails down convincingly truths which is has been sought illuminate.

MAGAZINES.

Though the January issue of The ntury is a "fiction number," the ef point of interest is the first two roductions in color made in Ameri- from the new color photographs by Lumiere process, the work of uard J. Steichen—transcriptions nirably indicating the subtlety, ige . and . beauty of the process, ich is the subject of an article by Nilsen Laurvik. The text as well the pictures will interest not only fessional photographers, but amateurs as well, and also the general public.

The fiction number is happily timed. It contains the beginning of Dr. S. Weir Mitchell's new novel, "The Red City," and short stories from May Sinclair, Jack London, Charles D. Stewart, David Gray, Barton W. Currie, Katherine Metcalf Roof, Roger A. Derby and Frances T. Lea—tragedy, pathos and humor being well balanced.

A new novel by Dr. S.' Weir Mitchell is always a cause for congratulation; and "The Red City" renews acquaintance with some of the characters and scenes of Dr. Mitchell's greatest success, "Hugh Wynne." The opening chapters tell, in the author's characteristic fashion, of the coming to Philadelphia, in the time of Washington's presidency, of a young Huguenot emigre and his widowed mother, and of their meeting with Hugh Wynne.

In this number, too, F. Marion Crawford tells the true story of Beatrice Cenci—"a great love-drama, less noble, but ever more human, and surely far more awful, than the 'Bride of Lammermoor' "—basing this new version of a long misunderstood tragedy, in part, upon some recently found valuable letters and documents not before published.

The topics of the times seem especially timely—"A 'Demonstration' by Governor Hughes," commending the State Executive's recent utterances on civil service reform; "A Good Working Hypothesis,". the doctrine that things are really getting better; "Mars: a New Phase," "Hard Times and Good Books."

It should be a Happy New Year surely for every youngster fortunate enough to have the January St. Nicholas, for a richer, fuller number of that children's magazine was never issued. It is almost a White House number— Chester M. Clark telling in much interesting detail of' "A Day's Work With the President," all the routine of one of President Roosevelt's busy days, while Jacob Riis relates the story of "Slippers, the White House Cat."

This first-of-the-year number brings the beginnings of three tempting new serials: Ralph Henry Barbour's "Harry's Island," continuing the fun and adventures of the old favorites of "Tom, Dick and Harriet;" Agnes McClelland Daulton's "The Gentle Interference of Bab," opening delightfully, and Carolyn Wells' and Harrison Cady's funny, very funny, "The Happy Chaps."

Besides all the jingles and pictures and departments, there are several exceptionally bright short stories, more chapters of the fascinating "Three Years Behind the Guns," General Howard's story of his experiences with the Indian Chief, Pascaul, and suggestions for lots of fun with "Butter-Dish Toys" in the new installment of "Hints and Helps for Mother."

ANNUAL MEETING OF THE AMERICAN FORESTRY ASSOCIATION.

The Annual Meeting of the American Forestry Association will be held in Washington, at the New Willard Hotel, on Wednesday, January 29, 1908, beginning at 10 o'clock A. M. On the evening of the same day a reception will be held at the residence of Mr. and Mrs. J. W. Pinchot and Mr. Gifford Pinchot, the Forester.

On arriving in Washington, members will be requested to register at Room 305 Epiphany Building, 1311 G Street, N. W.—the offices of the American Forestry Association. Programs and invitations to the reception will be issued at the time and place of registration.

Fittsylvania Co., Va., Sept. 23, '07.

I like the Southern Planter very much.   J. W. NEAL.

A Neat Binder for your back numbers can be had for 30 cents. Address our Business Department.

CONTENTS.

TWO BIG BANKRUPT STOCKS.

A big opportunity to buy VEHICLES, FARM WAGONS, HARNESS, PLOWS, AGRICULUTRAL IMPLEMENTS, FARM FENCING, AIR-TIGHT HEATERS, SEWING MACHINES, BABY CARRIAGES, Etc. Partial Price-List Below.

To add to our list of customers, we have purchased and now offer for sale two especially large bankrupt stocks which were bought by us at forced sales. Every article is absolutely new and all are of high-grade goods. Every purchaser has the right to return any goods not satisfactory, and we bind ourselves to return his money and pay freight charges both ways. Orders should be made from this advertisement, and we can furnish illustrations of most of the articles listed, and will gladly give any additional information desired. As a reference we refer you to the Bank of Richmond, Richmond, Va., or to the editor of this paper.

BUGGIES AND CARRIAGES.

Open Runabouts.

Seven Enger Road Wagons; body 24 inches wide; 15-16-inch long distance arch axles; 3 plate elliptic spring; wheels ¾-inch tread, 38-42 inches in diameter; body painted black and gear Brewster green. Regular price, $45. Our price $33 40

Five Enger Runabouts; body 23 inches wide; axle and springs same as above; ⅞-inch tread; wheels 40 and 44 inches; sarven patent wheels; body black; gear Brewster green; genuine leather trimmings. These Rigs are Enger's highest grades and sell anywhere for $70. Our price..$51 00

Six Concord Road Wagons, without top; body 29 inches wide; seat measures 34 inches across top of cushion; ample room behind seat; 1 1-16-inch long distance axles; 5 plate springs; body black; gear yellow; genuine leather trimmings. A very substantial business man's rig. Regular price, $75. Our price....................$52 00

TOP BUGGIES.

Fifteen Enger Top Buggies; body 20 inches wide; either 3 or 4 bow tops, as desired; 15-16 steel axle; wheels ¾-inch tread, 40 and 44 inches in diameter; all bodies black, but either Brewster green or red running gear, as may be desired. Our price only....................$42 00

Nine Enger Top Buggies; 24-inch bodies; 15-16 long distance axles; ¾-inch tread, either 2½ or 3 inch bow tops; genuine leather trimming throughout; Brewster green gear and black body. Regular $70 grade. Our price......$48.50

Seven Side-Spring Top Buggies; body 24 inches wide, 15-16 inches long distance steel axles; the celebrated Victor 4-plate side spring; body black and gear Brewster green; genuine leather trimmings. Selling price, $75.00. Our price $53 00

Phaetons, seat 31 inches across top of cushion; axles as above; ⅞-inch tread; wheels 36-44 inches in diameter; genuine leather trimmings throughout; body black and gear Brewster green. Regular price $85.00. Our price....$68 00

FARM WAGONS.

One-Horse Farm Wagons.

Seventeen 1¼-inch Steel Axle Wagons; tire 1¼x5-16 inches; front wheels 3 feet 4 inches; rear wheels 3 feet 10 inches; Sarven patent hubs; guaranteed capacity 1,500 pounds. These wagons were made by the Taylor Wagon Company, Lynchburg, Va., and are their standard wagons. Regular price, $32. Our price, complete with body and spring seat....................$26 00

Our price, gear only....................$22 00

Fourteen Russell One-Horse 2⅜-inch Thimble-Skein Wagons; tire 1¼x5-16; front wheels 3 feet 2 inches; rear wheels 3¼x8 inches. Capacity 2,000 pounds. Regular price $32. Our price, complete with body and spring seat..$27 00

Gear only, our price....................$23 50

The above wagons were made by Charles H. Russell & Son, Clarksville, Va., and are absolutely standard.

TWO-HORSE FARM WAGONS.

Nine 3-inch Thimble-Skein Taylor Wagons; tire 1⅝x⅝ inches; guaranteed capacity 3,000 pounds. Regular price $60.00. Our price complete with body and spring seat.$45 00

Gear only....................$36 00

Twenty-three Russell 2¾-inch Thimble-Skein Wagons; 1½x7-16-inch tire; capacity 2,500 pounds. Regular $55.00 grade. Our price, complete with body and spring seat.$44 00

Gear only....................$38 00

The above wagons were made by C. H. Russell & Son, Clarksville, Va., and are their standard wagons.

HEAVY THREE OR FOUR-HORSE FARM WAGONS.

Five 1¾-inch Steel Axle Taylor Wagons; tires 3x⅝-inch; guaranteed capacity 4,500 pounds; weight 1,000 pounds. Regular $75.00 grade. Our price....................$55 00

Price of gear only....................$47 00

TWO SEAT RIGS.

Twelve Dayton Wagons With Canopy Top; two seats, both removable; 1-inch tread; axles 1 1-16 steel; oil tempered elliptic springs; drop end gate; leather trimmings, either with black body and gear or finished in natural wood throughout. Former price was $75.00. Now..........$56 00

Five Canopy Top Surries, back seat removable; seat measures 33 inches across top of cushion; 1 1-16 steel long distance axle; 4 plate elliptic springs; 1-inch tread; genuine leather trimmings; body black; gear Brewster green; complete with side curtains. Regular price $80.00. Now..$62 00

Four Two-Seated Open Three-Spring Wagons; body 34 inches wide; 80 inches long with removable seats; wheels 1-inch tread; 38 and 42 inches in diameter; genuine leather trimmings; body black; gear red. A very handy wagon. Made by Frank J. Enger Company. Sells anywhere for $65.00. Now....................$48 50

SOUTH BEND STEEL-BEAM PLOWS.

These are the genuine Steel-Beam South Bend Plow, made at South Bend, Indiana, and this is the lowest price ever put upon this well-known plow. We can furnish the parts for the above plow at equally low prices.

20 No. 1 F One-Horse. Regular price, $4.50. Our price $3 25

10 No. 2½ F Light Two-Horse. Regular price $7.00. Our price $5 25

12 No. 3 F Two-Horse. Turns 10 to 12 inches; each once $8.00. Our price....................$6 00

5 No. 4 F Heavy Two-Horse. Turns 11 to 13 inches; each once $8.50. Our price....................$6 00

5 No. 10 A Three-Horse; turns 11½ to 14 inches; each once $9.00. Our price....................$7 00

173 S. B. Plow Standards; any size; once $1.25. Now, each ....75 cents.

Forty-five Sets Extra Buggy Shafts. Well seasoned hickory stock. Regular price $5.00. Our price........$2 50

Forty-three South Bend Double Shovels; width of cut 20 inches; beams of plows are made of 1¾x¾-inch steel; shovels are 6 inches wide, 11 inches long. Regular price $2.50. Our price....................$1 70

HARNESS.

Eighty Sets Single Buggy Harness, made by Cottrell Saddlery Company, Richmond, Va.

Saddle—Three-inch strap, fancy or plain bound, nickel or brass trimmed, shaft tugs; 1-inch double and stitched girth, Griffith; 1¼-inch, single leather, ¾-inch point; turnback ¾x1-inch, plain; round dock; hip strap, ⅝-inch flat, plain finish; breeching 1⅜-inch; single leather ⅞-inch tug; ½-inch stay; 1-inch lay; breeching straps; ¾-inch bar buckles; breast collar and traces; cut-out breast collar, 2¾x1⅛ inches; traces sewed to breast collar; bridle ⅝x1 inch; flat winker braced; reins ⅞x¾ inches, with snap sewed; trimming, nickel or brass; bar buckles........$7 50

If Collar and Hames are wanted in place of breast collar we can furnish black collar, ⅛-inch traces, single strap, and ⅛-inch box loop tug on hames....................$9 70

Shipping weight in case about 25 pounds.

This Harness is their standard $15.00 Harness.

ROLLERS, CULTIVATORS, ETC.

Fifteen Genuine Southern Disc Harrows, made by Thomas Manufacturing Company, Springfield, O. These Harrows are 10 disc, 20 inches in diameter, have all modern improvements. We can furnish illustration and full particulars. Regular price $24.00. Our price, without double trees and single trees $16 00

With double trees and single trees....................$18 00

Twelve Roderick Lean Hand Rollers, 24-inch drums, highest grade made.

Six-foot, 2 section roller, 570 pounds....................$16 50

Eight-foot, 3 section roller, 725 pounds....................$19 00

Nine One-Horse Roderick Lean Seed Drills, with both seed and fertilizer attachment. The highest grade seed drill made.

Disc Drill (5 disc)....................$19 00

Shoe Drill (5 shoes)....................$14 00

Seven National Two-Horse Riding Double-Row Cultivator. Regular price, $50.00. Now....................$35 00

Twelve National Riding Single Row Cultivators. Has 8 shovels, thoroughly adjustable and latest pattern. Regular price $30.00. Now....................$18 00

Five Cassidy Foot Left Riding Plows; cuts 14 inches. The highest grade Riding Plow made. Sells anywhere for $50.00. Our price....................$30 00

One hundred and fifty Short Handle Genuine Steel Shovels, either square or round point. Regular price 65 cents. Now ....35 cents.

TERMS.

All prices are based on cash with the order, but if any one will deposit the amount of his purchase with his bank and they will write us he has done this, we will ship the goods C. O. D., subject to his examination before paying a cent on them. MOREOVER, WE BIND OURSELVES TO TAKE BACK ANYTHING NOT SATISFACTORY AND TO AT ONCE REFUND PRICE AND ALL TRANSPORTATION CHARGES PAID. All goods will be shipped from Richmond, and the samples of this stock can be seen at our warehouse. We, of course, reserve the privilege of withdrawing these prices as soon as this particular stock is exhausted.

SPOTLESS CO., INC., 122 SHOCKOE SQUARE **RICHMOND, VA.**

Lightning Source UK Ltd.
Milton Keynes UK
UKHW020621060119
334855UK00006B/477/P